Scope & Sequence

Year 1: Fall	Year 1: Winter	Year 1: Spring	Year 1: Summer	Year 2: Fall
UNIT 1: Beginnings Genesis 1:31	**UNIT 1: Hope** Isaiah 2:5	**UNIT 1: Journey** Psalm 121:8	**UNIT 1: Paul** Philippians 4:13	**UNIT 1: Joseph** Jeremiah 29:11
1. Creation Genesis 1:1-25	1. Swords into Plows Isaiah 2:1-5	1. Man in the Synagogue Matthew 12:9-14	1. Paul's Conversion Acts 9:1-20	1. Joseph and His Brothers Genesis 37:1-36
2. God's Image Genesis 1:26–2:4a	2. Mary's Story Luke 1:26-38, 46-47	2. Jesus and the Children Matthew 19:13-15	2. Love in Action Romans 12:9-18	2. Joseph in Egypt Genesis 39:1–40:23
3. Adam and Eve Genesis 2:4b–3:24	3. Joseph's Story Matthew 1:18-24	3. Last Supper Matthew 26:17-30	3. Paul Escapes Acts 9:20-25	3. Joseph Saves the Day Genesis 41:1-57
4. Noah Genesis 6:1–9:17	4. Jesus' Story Luke 2:1-7	4. In the Garden Matthew 26:31-56	4. Be Glad and Endure Philippians 4:4-14	4. Joseph and His Brothers Reunite Genesis 42:1–46:34
5. Tower of Babel Genesis 11:1-9	5. Shepherds' Story Luke 2:8-20	5. Peter Matthew 26:57-58, 69-75		
UNIT 2: Ancestors Genesis 15:5	**UNIT 2: Calling** Matthew 4:19	**UNIT 2: Alleluia** Matthew 28:7	**UNIT 2: Leaders** 2 Timothy 1:7	**UNIT 2: Exodus** Exodus 3:12
6. Abraham and Sarah Genesis 12:1-9; 15:1-6	6. Follow the Star Matthew 2:1-12	6. Hosanna! Matthew 21:1-11; 27:32-66	5. Timothy Is Chosen Acts 16:1-5; 1 Timothy 4:7b-16	5. The Baby in the Basket Exodus 1:8–2:10
7. Abraham and Lot Genesis 13:1-12	7. Jesus Is Baptized Matthew 3:13-17	7. Easter Matthew 28:1-10	6. Be Encouraged Timothy 1:3-7	6. The Burning Bush Exodus 2:11–3:22
8. The Birth of Isaac Genesis 18:1-15; 21:1-7	8. Jesus Calls the Fishermen Matthew 4:18-22	8. Breakfast on the Beach John 21:1-19	7. Lydia Acts 16:11-15	7. Moses and Pharaoh Exodus 5:1–13:9
9. Isaac and Rebekah Genesis 24:1-67	9. Beatitudes Matthew 5:1-12	9. The Great Commission Matthew 28:16-20	8. Paul and Silas Acts 16:16-40	8. Crossing the Sea Exodus 13:17–14:31
UNIT 3: Blessings Genesis 28:14	**UNIT 3: Wisdom** Matthew 7:24	**UNIT 3: Believers** Acts 2:4	**UNIT 3: Prophets** 1 Kings 18:39	**UNIT 2: Wilderness** Exodus 15:2
10. Jacob and Esau Genesis 25:19-28	10. The Lord's Prayer Matthew 6:5-15	10. Believers Share Acts 4:32-37	9. Elijah and the Ravens 1 Kings 16:29-30; 17:1-7	9. Songs of Joy Exodus 15:1-21
11. The Birthright Genesis 25:29-34	11. The Birds in the Sky Matthew 6:25-34	11. Choosing the Seven Acts 6:1-7	10. Elijah and the Prophets 1 Kings 18:20-39	10. In the Wilderness Exodus 15:22–17:7
12. The Blessing Genesis 27:1-46	12. The Golden Rule Matthew 7:12	12. Philip and the Ethiopian Acts 8:26-40	11. Elijah and Elisha 1 Kings 19:1-21	11. Ten Commandments Exodus 19:1–20:21
13. Jacob's Dream Genesis 28:10-22	13. The Two Houses Matthew 7:24-27	13. First Called "Christians" Acts 11:19-30	12. Elisha and the Widow 2 Kings 4:1-7	12. A House for God Exodus 25:1–31:18; 35:4–40:38
		14. Pentecost Acts 2:1-41	13. Elisha and Naaman 2 Kings 5:1-19a	13. Elizabeth and Zechariah Luke 1:5-25

Contents

- 2 Welcome to Bible Story Basics
- 3 What Children Ages 3-7 Need
- 4 Using This Leader Guide
- 5 Resources
- 6 Supplies

UNIT 1: Journey
- 7 **Session 1**
  Man in the Synagogue
- 13 **Session 2**
  Jesus and the Children
- 19 **Session 3**
  Last Supper
- 25 **Session 4**
  In the Garden
- 31 **Session 5**
  Peter

UNIT 2: Alleluia
- 37 **Session 6**
  Hosanna!
- 43 **Session 7**
  Easter
- 49 **Session 8**
  Breakfast on the Beach
- 55 **Session 9**
  The Great Commission

UNIT 3: Believers
- 61 **Session 10**
  Believers Share
- 67 **Session 11**
  Choosing the Seven
- 73 **Session 12**
  Philip and the Ethiopian
- 79 **Session 13**
  First Called "Christians"
- 85 **Session 14**
  Pentecost

Supplemental Pages
- 91 Song Lyrics
- 87 Bible Verse Signs
- 96 Comments from Users

Bible STORY BASICS

- unleashes the power of God's Word to work in the minds and hearts of children;
- establishes the Bible as foundational in children's lives and faith;
- equips both leaders and children to read, appreciate, and understand Scripture and its historical context and enduring message; and
- provides children a depth of spiritual resources to draw upon in difficult times.

Check out
www.biblestorybasics.com
to stay up to date on all the
Bible Story Basics news.

Cover illustrations by Ralph Voltz, cover design by Ed Maksimowicz.

Art—p. 12: Eva Vagreti; pp. 18, 36, 55, 60, 84: Shutterstock; p. 23: Carol Schwartz; pp. 30, 42, 48: Dan Sharp; pp. 66, 78, 90: Craig Cameron; p. 72: Jim Padgett; pp. 93, 94, 95: Diana Magnuson.

Welcome to

We're glad you're here! This year you and your kids will journey together to discover tools for reading and learning the Bible. Your children will hear foundational Bible stories, memorize key verses, and internalize God's Word while having fun with music, games, puzzles, prayer, and more!

BIBLE STORY BASICS is a comprehensive three-year Bible study built to help children understand the overarching story of God's Word while nurturing and growing their faith—without a lot of complicated extras.

With a simple look and feel, these lessons are straightforward and easy to teach. The broad age-level structure (ages 3–7 and 8–12) makes it simple to group your children, while also providing leaders the confidence to teach age-appropriate lessons.

We invite you and your children to experience the depths of God's love expressed in the stories of the Bible. It's basic!

What Children Ages 3–7 Need

For developing faith foundations, children need	For knowing the Bible and our faith traditions, children need	For relating to God and the church, children need	For relating faith to daily living, children need
• to be with adults whose Christian attitudes and behaviors the children can imitate; • to have their feelings and actions accepted and to be forgiven when they do not meet adult expectations; • to develop and express their own identity as individuals and in relation to others; • to be guided in playing cooperatively with other children; and • to practice decision-making through optional activities.	• to handle the Bible and see others read from it; • to sing and say Bible verses, especially from Psalms and the Gospels; • to recognize the Lord's Prayer, the Golden Rule, and other affirmations of our faith; • to hear stories of Bible people who lived as God wanted them to live; • to participate in Communion with parents or other caregivers; and • to hear short stories about the church today and in the past.	• to learn simple prayers; • to be encouraged to give their own offerings to God and to the church; • to develop a sense of belonging at church and of being a child of God; • to have accepting adults who are willing to hear their many questions about God, life, death, and crises; and • to experience awe and wonder through nature, life cycles, and corporate worship, even though they may not be able to talk about the meanings of their experiences.	• to hear stories about service to others and to observe leaders, parents, and older children in service to others; • to participate in service by making things for others and by sharing money and food; • to hear leaders, parents, or guardians pray about people and situations beyond themselves; • to use Sunday school take-home items as reminders of what they learned in Sunday school; and • to practice caring for and appreciating God's world.

Using This Leader Guide

Underlying each aspect of the BIBLE STORY BASICS curriculum is the belief that all children should have the opportunity to experience the depths of God's love for them expressed in the timeless stories of the Bible. Each story-focused session allows the narrative to drive children's faith formation and provides a rich context for the development of biblical literacy skills.

Bible Background and Devotion

The first page of each Leader Guide session offers Bible background and a devotion to help the facilitator prepare for the lesson, better understand the biblical context, and spend a few moments in meditation and prayer.

Lesson Flow

B — The flow of the lesson starts with **Bible Beginnings**. This is the time to welcome the children and introduce the Bible story. Each week the pre-readers will have a coloring picture of the Bible story and a Bible puzzle. There is also a suggestion for Bible play. Play is an important way young children learn. This activity will focus their play on the Bible story.

I — The lesson then moves **Into the Bible**. This will include two opportunities for the children to hear the Bible story, one from the *Bible Basics Storybook,* and one from the week's Bible Story Leaflet. The leaflet story will be interactive. This section will also include the Bible tool, helping the children learn the Bible verse and the mechanics of the Bible.

B — Following the Bible story, the children will experience activities that help them make **Bible Connections**. These activities draw from various learning styles to present age-appropriate ideas and help deepen the children's understanding of the Bible story.

L — Next, the lesson moves to activities that will help the children **Live the Bible** and make the Bible relevant to their own lives.

E — Finally, the lesson will close with opportunities to **Express Praise**. This section includes a song and prayer, plus suggestions for how you can bless and affirm each child.

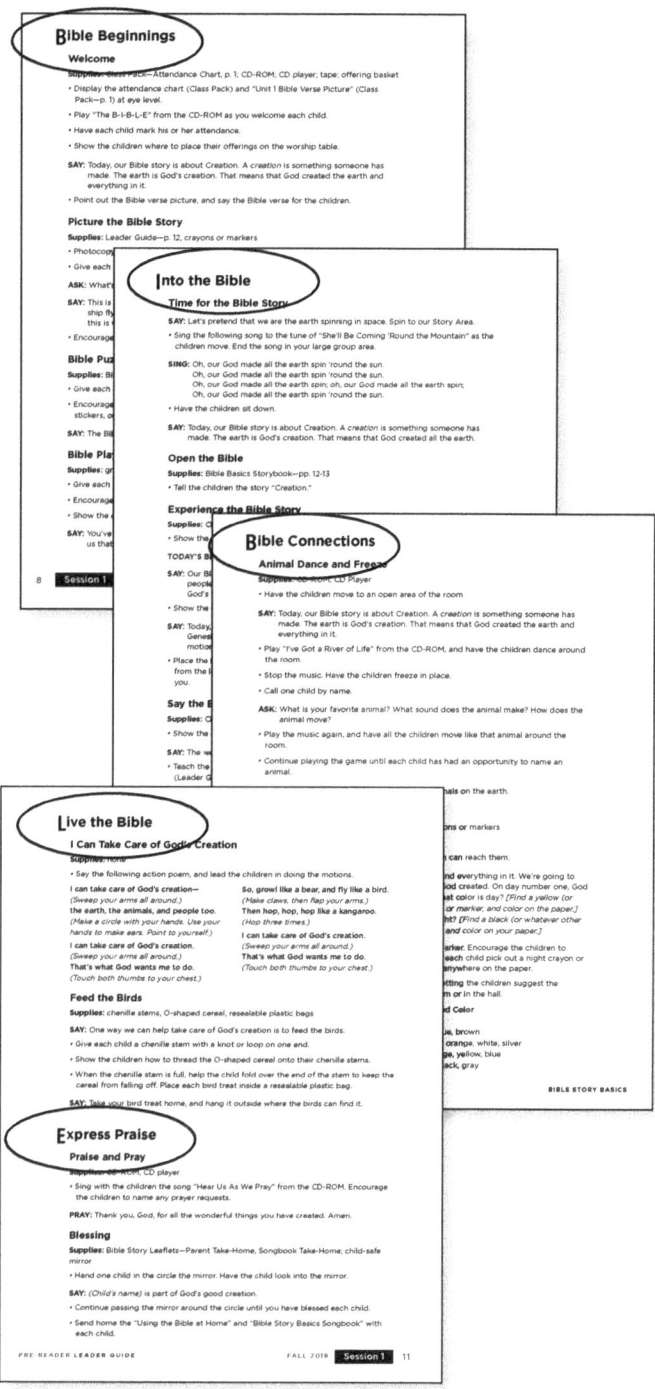

Resources

Leader Guide

This guide features 14 low-prep and step-by-step session guides that offer creative ways for children to experience foundational Bible stories through a variety of learning styles.

Bible Story Leaflets

These leaflets feature colorful and realistic art from Ralph Voltz and offer creative ways to involve children in the Bible story and to facilitate a connection between church and home with weekly questions and prayers to share as a family.

Class Pack

The annual Class Pack includes 12 Bible verse pictures to assist in Scripture memorization, a CD-ROM containing music and additional teaching materials, and an Attendance Chart. The additional teaching materials on the CD-ROM are also available to download at *biblestorybasics.com/resources*.

Student Take-Home CD

This CD includes seven memorable songs for the children to learn and enjoy throughout the year. The CD is sold in packs of five at a price that makes it possible to send one home with each child.

Bible Basics Storybook

The 149 Old and New Testament stories in this storybook will invite your child into the Word through beautiful illustrations, retellings that are appropriate for young children, and prayers that connect to our faith.

BIBLE STORY BASICS resources are available in Braille on request.

Contact:
Braille Ministry
c/o Donna Veigel
10810 N. 91st Avenue #96
Peoria, AZ 85345
623-979-7552

Supplies

No matter what activities you choose to use, there are some basic supplies you likely will need at some point. Collect these supplies and keep them accessible every Sunday.

The Basics

- baby dolls
- CD player
- CEB Bibles
- chenille stems
- child-safe mirrors
- clear tape
- construction paper
- cotton balls
- crayons
- glue
- markers
- masking tape
- newsprint
- offering basket
- paper bowls
- paper cups
- paper plates
- pencils
- plain paper
- plastic table covering
- play dough
- posterboard
- scissors
- spoons
- stapler
- star stickers
- tray
- washable paint

Beyond the Basics

Once you have chosen the activities in each session that you intend to do, check the specific supplies for each activity.

If some of the necessary supplies are slightly out of the ordinary, make a wish list of the supplies you will need. Publish the list in the church newsletter or bulletin. Members of your church will be happy to know how they can support the children in the church.

If you have a place to store supplies, encourage the congregation to bring the supplies you will need for the rest of the quarter. If you do not have a place to store things, make a new list each week of the things you will need in the next two or three weeks.

 SPRING YEAR 1

Man in the Synagogue

Bible Verse: The Lord will protect you on your journeys—whether going or coming. (Psalm 121:8)

Bible Story: Matthew 12:9-14

Bible Background

An important part of today's story is the first-century Jewish understanding of the Sabbath. The Sabbath was commanded by God in the Ten Commandments (Exodus 20:8-11) and was also blessed by God at the Creation (Genesis 2:3). The celebration of the Sabbath separated the Jews from the Gentiles and was a witness to the Jewish belief in one God.

At the time of Jesus, there was a debate about how the Sabbath law was to be interpreted. Some rabbis taught that an animal that fell into a pit on the Sabbath could be helped out. Others said the sheep must stay in the pit. Some Jews thought it was OK to heal on the Sabbath. Others thought that healing could take place only if the person was in danger of dying.

When Jesus entered the synagogue in today's story, he was watched by Pharisees. Pharisees were a Jewish sect who dedicated themselves to preserving the purity of the Jewish faith. They were often critical of Jesus because he seemed to ignore the traditions they believed were so important.

When Jesus encountered the man with the withered hand, the Pharisees asked, "Does the Law allow a person to heal on the Sabbath?" (Matthew 12:10). The Pharisees wanted to accuse Jesus of violating Sabbath law. Jesus responds by pointing out that God's love and care is more important than observing the law: "So the Law allows a person to do what is good on the Sabbath" (Matthew 12:12). This answer angered the Pharisees, and they began the plot to kill Jesus.

Devotion

As followers of Jesus, we follow Jesus' example. Few of us have the power to heal as Jesus did. However, we each have the power to do good. We can show love to people all the time, on any day of the week, just as Jesus did. You show love to children when you teach them, either on Sunday or another weekday. What else can you do this week to show love to someone?

BASIC

Plan

Bible Beginnings
- Welcome
- Picture the Bible Story
- Bible Puzzle
- Bible Play

Into the Bible
- Time for the Bible Story
- Open the Bible
- Experience the Bible Story
- Say the Bible Verse

Bible Connections
- Can You Do It with Only One Hand?
- It's Time to Help

Live the Bible
- Our Hands Help Others
- Wrap It Up

Express Praise
- Praise and Pray
- Blessing

Bible Beginnings

Welcome

Supplies: Class Pack—Attendance Chart, p. 7; CD-ROM; CD player; tape; offering basket

- Display the Attendance Chart (Class Pack) and "Unit 1 Bible Verse Picture" (Class Pack—p. 7) at the children's eye level.
- Play, "The B-I-B-L-E" (CD-ROM), as you welcome each child.
- Show the children where to place their offerings on the worship table.

SAY: In our Bible story today, Jesus went to the synagogue and saw a man with a hurt hand. A synagogue is a special place to worship God.

- Point out the Bible Verse Picture, and say the Bible verse for the child.

Picture the Bible Story

Supplies: Leader Guide—p. 12, crayons or markers

- Photocopy "Jesus Heals" for each child.
- Give each child a copy of the picture.

SAY: In our Bible story today, Jesus went to the synagogue and saw a man with a hurt hand. A synagogue is a special place to worship God.

- Encourage the children to find twelve hidden objects in the picture of Jesus, the healed man, and the Pharisees.
- Have each child circle the hidden objects and color the picture.

Bible Puzzle

Supplies: Bible Story Leaflet—Session 1, p. 4; crayons or markers

- Give each child a copy of "Ways We Worship."
- Encourage each child to draw a line between the matching pictures.

SAY: On the Sabbath, Jesus went to the synagogue to worship God.

ASK: What are some of the ways we can worship God at our church?

Bible Play

Supplies: blocks

- Invite the children to use the blocks to make a synagogue or a church.

SAY: Our Bible story today is about a man with a hurt hand. Jesus met the man when they were at the synagogue on the Sabbath. A synagogue is a special place to worship God. The Sabbath is a special day to worship God.

ASK: What is the name of the special place we go to worship God. *(church)* What is the name of the special day we come to church to worship God? *(Sunday)*

Into the Bible

Time for the Bible Story

SAY: Let's pretend we're going to the synagogue with Jesus.

- Invite the children to follow you to your story area. Sing the song printed below to the tune of "Mary Had a Little Lamb" as you lead the children.

SING: Let's go to the synagogue, synagogue, synagogue.
    Let's go to the synagogue,
  a place to worship God.

- Have the children sit down.

SAY: In our Bible story today, Jesus went to the synagogue and saw a man with a hurt hand. A synagogue is a special place to worship God.

Open the Bible

Supplies: Bible Basics Storybook—pp. 154-155

- Tell the children the story, "Man in the Synagogue."

Experience the Bible Story

Supplies: CEB Bible; Bible Story Leaflet—Session 1, pp. 2-3

- Show the children the Bible.

TODAY'S BIBLE TOOL: Matthew is the first book in the New Testament.

SAY: Our Bible has two parts: the Old Testament and the New Testament. The two parts are divided into books. Today's story is from the Book of Matthew, the first book in the New Testament.

- Show the children the Book of Matthew.

SAY: Today our story is from Matthew, chapter 12.

- Show the children Matthew 12. Place your Leaflet inside the Bible as you tell the story.

SAY: Listen and watch as I tell the story. Do the motions with me.

- Tell the children the story, "Man in the Synagogue" from the Bible Story Leaflet, and encourage them to repeat the refrain and do the motions.

ASK: How do you think the man felt when Jesus healed the man's hand? Do you think it was OK for Jesus to heal the man on the Sabbath?

Say the Bible Verse

Supplies: Class Pack—p. 7, Leader Guide—p. 93

- Show the children the Bible Verse Picture. Repeat the verse for the children.
- Teach the children signs from American Sign Language (Leader Guide) to go along with the verse.
- Encourage the children to make the signs as they say the verse again.

Bible Connections

Can You Do It with Only One Hand?

Supplies: paper, boxes or containers of crayons

- Have the children try to do some activities using only one of their hands.

- Place a stack of plain paper on the table, along with boxes or containers of crayons. Have each child try to pick up a piece of paper and place it on the table. Then have each child try to open the box of crayons and pull out a crayon. Finally, have the child sit down and color the paper—all using only one hand.

- You might also have the children take off their shoes and then try to put their shoes back on and fasten them—again, using only one hand.

SAY: In our Bible story today, Jesus healed a man who had a hurt hand.

ASK: How do you think the man felt when he was only able to use one hand to get dressed, eat, and work? How do you think the man felt when Jesus healed his hand? What do you think was the first thing the man did using both his hands?

TIP: If you have a child who has the use of only one hand, let the child show and talk about all the things he or she can do.

It's Time to Help

Supplies: none

- Have the children move to an open area of the room.

- Choose a child to be the timekeeper. Have the timekeeper stand on one side of the room, facing the other side of the room.

- Have the rest of the children stand on the opposite side of the room, facing the timekeeper.

SAY: Let's play a game: "It's Time to Help." All of you except the timekeeper will say together, "What time is it, timekeeper?" The timekeeper will say, "It's two o'clock," or whatever time the timekeeper chooses. You will each count off the number of steps that correspond to what time it is. Then you will ask the question again. The timekeeper will respond again, and you will move again. At some point, the timekeeper will say, "It's time to help!" That is your cue to turn around and run back to your side of the room. The timekeeper will chase you and tag someone to be the new timekeeper.

ASK: When did Jesus heal the man with the hurt hand? *(on the Sabbath)*

SAY: There were rules that said you should not work on the Sabbath. Some people thought that it was wrong for Jesus to heal on the Sabbath because it was a kind of work.

ASK: Do you think Jesus should have healed the man on the Sabbath?

SAY: Yes! Any time is a good time to help others.

Live the Bible

Our Hands Help Others

Supplies: construction paper, pencils, markers, tape, scissors

ASK: What do you think the man did after Jesus healed his hand? How can you use your hands to help others?

SAY: Let's make a wreath with our helping hands.

- Encourage the children to trace and cut out their hands. Younger children may need help with tracing and cutting.
- Invite the children to write or draw a way to help others on each hand.
- Collect the hands and place them in a circle, overlapping like a wreath. Place them so the words and drawings can be seen. Tape the hands together.
- Hang the wreath on a door so others can see all the ways children can help others.

SAY: We can't heal like Jesus, but there are many ways we can help others.

Wrap It Up

Supplies: elastic bandages

- Encourage the children to wrap bandages around each other's arms and hands.

SAY: We can't heal the way Jesus did, but we can do things to help others feel better.

Express Praise

Praise and Pray

Supplies: CD-ROM, CD player

- Sing with the children the song, "Hear Us As We Pray," from the CD-ROM.
- Encourage the children to name any prayer requests.

PRAY: Thank you, God, for Jesus and all the ways we can help others. Amen.

Blessing

Supplies: Songbook Leaflet, Family Devotions Leaflet: Open My Eyes

- Have all the children face one side of the room.

SAY: If you journey this way, God is with you. *(Have the children turn to face the opposite side of the room.)* If you journey this way, God is with you.

- Call each child by name.

SAY: *(Child's name)*, God is always with you. *(Continue until you have blessed each child.)*

TIP: Send the Family Devotions Leaflet: Open My Eyes and the Songbook Leaflet home with each child. Keep one copy of the Songbook Leaflet in the classroom.

Jesus Heals

Look at the picture of Jesus, the healed man, and the Pharisees. Can you find the hidden items? Check the list of items at the bottom of the picture to help you know what to look for.

money bag, oil lamp, ceremonial shovel, keys, scroll, sparrow, 3 loaves of bread, lampstand, pitcher, goblet, bowl, basket

The LORD will protect you on your journeys—whether going or coming.
Psalm 121:8

Jesus and the Children

Bible Verse: The Lord will protect you on your journeys—whether going or coming. (Psalm 121:8)

Bible Story: Matthew 19:13-15

Bible Background

In today's lesson, we'll explore the familiar Bible story of Jesus blessing the children. The disciples tried to keep the children from Jesus. Children can certainly relate to being told not to do something. Every child has had this experience. As you teach this week's lesson, help your children think about how they feel when they are not allowed to do something that they want to do (even if there is a good reason for the restriction). Help the children imagine how the children must have felt when they were not allowed to go to Jesus.

We're not told why the parents were bringing their children to Jesus. In those days, the infant mortality rate was high. Many children died before reaching the age of sixteen. It is likely the parents had heard of Jesus' healing miracles and wanted him to bless and protect their children.

When the disciples attempted to discourage the parents from bringing their children to see Jesus, they weren't intentionally being mean to children. They were acting in a way consistent with the social norms of the time. Children were considered to be their father's property, not persons in their own right. Children were without status. Thus, children should not be allowed to disturb Jesus while he was teaching.

When Jesus reprimanded the disciples for keeping the children away, he made a clear statement that access to him and to God's love was for everyone. There are no "non-persons" in God's kingdom. By blessing children, Jesus showed they were full members of God's family.

Jesus used the children as an example to teach the disciples about the kingdom of God. Jesus said that we must receive the kingdom as a child. Some people refer to the coming kingdom of God, alluding to a time in the future when Jesus will return. However, during his ministry, Jesus taught that the Kingdom is a present reality (Luke 17:20-21).

Devotion

Take time to read Dr. Seuss's book, "Horton Hears a Who." Enjoy the message that "a person is a person no matter how small." Share the book with a child you know. Affirm to the children in your class that they are an integral part of God's family and your church family.

BASIC

Plan

Bible Beginnings
Welcome
Picture the Bible Story
Bible Puzzle
Bible Play

Into the Bible
Time for the Bible Story
Open the Bible
Experience the Bible Story
Say the Bible Verse

Bible Connections
J E S U S
Jesus, May I?

Live the Bible
Jesus Loves
Blessing Medallions

Express Praise
Praise and Pray
Blessing

Bible Beginnings

Welcome

Supplies: Class Pack—Attendance Chart, p. 7; CD-ROM; CD player; tape; offering basket

- Display the Attendance Chart (Class Pack) and "Unit 1 Bible Verse Picture" (Class Pack—p. 7) at the children's eye level.
- Play, "The B-I-B-L-E" (CD-ROM), as you welcome each child.
- Show the children where to place their offerings on the worship table.

SAY: In our Bible story today, parents were bringing their children to see Jesus.

- Point out the Bible Verse Picture, and say the Bible verse for the child.

Picture the Bible Story

Supplies: Leader Guide—p. 18, crayons or markers

- Photocopy "Jesus and the Children" for each child.
- Give each child a copy of the picture.

SAY: In our Bible story today, parents were bringing their children to see Jesus. Jesus' helpers tried to stop the children, but Jesus wanted the children to come to him.

- Encourage each child to decorate the picture with crayons or markers.

Bible Puzzle

Supplies: Bible Story Leaflet—Session 2, p. 4; crayons or markers

- Give each child a copy of "Jesus and the Children."
- Encourage the children to use a finger or a crayon to trace the path from the children to Jesus.

SAY: In our Bible story today, parents were bringing their children to see Jesus.

Bible Play

Supplies: magnets, metal and plastic paper clips, metal and plastic lids, cookie tray, table

- Place things that contain iron (such as metal paper clips and metal lids) and things that don't contain iron (such as plastic paper clips and plastic lids) on a cookie tray.
- Place magnets beside the tray.
- Let the children experiment with the magnets. Help them discover that magnets *attract* (or pull) things with iron, such as metal paper clips and lids. Help them discover that magnets *repel* (or push away) things that don't have iron, such as plastic paper clips and plastic lids.

SAY: In our Bible story, parents were bringing their children to see Jesus. Jesus was a "magnet." He attracted children. They wanted to see him. Jesus helps us know that God loves each one of us.

Into the Bible

Time for the Bible Story

SAY: Let's pretend we are the children going to see Jesus.

- Have the children line up behind you. Say the following action rhyme as you march around the room. End the poem in your story area.

SING: Let's go marching, marching, marching, all around the town.
  Let's go marching, marching, marching, up the hills and down.
  Let's go marching, marching, marching, 'cause marching is such fun.
  Let's go marching, marching, marching to Jesus, God's own Son.

- Have the children sit down.

Open the Bible

Supplies: Bible Basics Storybook—pp. 156–157

- Tell the children the story, "Jesus and the Children."

Experience the Bible Story

Supplies: CEB Bible; Bible Story Leaflet—Session 2, pp. 2-3

- Show the children the Bible.

TODAY'S BIBLE TOOL: Stories about Jesus are in the New Testament.

SAY: Our Bible has many stories. Some of the stories tell about the beginnings of God's people. These stories are in the Old Testament. Some of the stories tell about God's Son, Jesus. These stories are in the New Testament.

- Show the children the beginning of the New Testament. Then show the children the Book of Matthew. Turn to the nineteenth chapter.

SAY: Today our story is the about what happened when parents brought their children to see Jesus. It is chapter nineteen in the Book of Matthew. Listen and watch as I tell the story. You can help me do some motions.

- Place the Leaflet in your Bible. Tell the children the story, "Jesus and the Children" from the Bible Story Leaflet, and encourage them to do the motions with you as suggested.

ASK: How do you think the children felt when Jesus' helpers stopped them from going to see Jesus? How do you think they felt when Jesus told them to come to him?

Say the Bible Verse

Supplies: Class Pack—p. 7, Leader Guide—p. 93

- Show the children the Bible Verse Picture. Repeat the verse for the children.
- Teach the children signs from American Sign Language (Leader Guide) to go along with the verse.
- Encourage the children to make the signs as they say the verse again.

Bible Connections

JESUS

Supplies: mural paper, permanent marker, heart stickers, crayons or markers, confetti or very small scraps of construction paper, glue

- Write the name J E S U S in large bubble letters across a piece of mural paper.

SAY: In our Bible story today, parents were bringing their children to see Jesus. Jesus' helpers were not sure the families should be able to see Jesus, but Jesus wanted the children to come to him. Jesus wanted the children to know they were important to God. Let's make a banner with Jesus' name.

- Encourage the children to decorate inside the letters with heart stickers and crayons or markers. The children may also glue on colorful confetti or very small pieces of construction paper around the letters.

- Sing the following song to the tune of "B-I-N-G-O" as the children work on the mural. Each time you repeat the verse, replace a letter of Jesus' name with a clap, until you are clapping in place of all five letters. (For example, on the first repetition, "J-E-S-U-S" will become "*(Clap)*-E-S-U-S.")

SING: Jesus says to us, "Come, follow me."
    Let's go and spell his name-o.
    J-E-S-U-S.
    J-E-S-U-S.
    J-E-S-U-S.
    And Jesus is his name-o.

Jesus, May I?

Supplies: J E S U S mural made earlier, tape

- Tape the J E S U S mural on one side of the room.
- Have the children line up on the opposite side of the room. You should stand in front of the mural.

SAY: Let's play, "Jesus, May I?" This game is like "Mother, May I?" I will pretend to be Jesus.

- Give directions to the children one at a time. For example, "Ginny, you may take one step forward."
- Wait for the player to respond. If she says, "Jesus, may I?" answer, "Yes, you may."
- Make sure the child asks the question and follows your instructions, but be gentle and always say yes. Jesus always responds to us with, "Yes, come closer," and we want to make sure the children get that message in the game.
- Continue giving commands to the children in any order you choose.
- Play until all of the children have made it to you, "Jesus."

SAY: Jesus always says yes. He wants everyone to come to him.

Live the Bible

Jesus Loves You

Supplies: beanbag (or pair of rolled-up socks), slips of paper, marker, basket

- Write each child's name on a slip of paper. Place all the names in a basket.
- Have the children sit in a circle on the floor. Show the children the basket of names.
- Toss the beanbag to someone in the circle. Have the person who catches the beanbag come to the basket and draw a name. Read the name out loud. Have the child who picked the slip of paper throw the beanbag to that child.
- Have everyone say, "Jesus loves *(name of person whose paper was drawn)*." Then have the first child sit down as the new child picks a name.
- Continue until everyone's name has been drawn.

Blessing Medallions

Supplies: yarn, heart stickers, construction paper, glue, crayons, markers, scissors

- Cut a heart about 3–4 inches large out of construction paper for each child. Each child will need two hearts. Cut yarn into 18-inch lengths.
- Give each child two hearts. Write "Jesus loves *(child's name)*" on one heart. Let each child decorate both hearts with heart stickers and crayons or markers.
- Have each child glue the two hearts back-to-back. This will make the heart medallion sturdier. Punch a hole in the top of the two hearts.
- Thread the yarn through the hole and tie the ends to make a necklace.
- Place each child's necklace over her or his head and say, "Jesus loves *(child's name)*."

Express Praise

Praise and Pray

Supplies: CD-ROM, CD player

- Sing with the children the song, "Hear Us As We Pray," from the CD-ROM. Encourage the children to name any prayer requests.

PRAY: Thank you, God, for all the wonderful things you have created. Amen.

Blessing

Supplies: none

- Have all the children face one side of the room.

SAY: If you journey this way, God is with you. *(Have the children turn to face the opposite side of the room.)* If you journey this way, God is with you. *(Call each child by name.)*

SAY: *(Child's name)*, God is always with you. *(Continue and bless each child.)*

Jesus and the Children

**The LORD will protect you on your journeys—whether going or coming.
Psalm 121:8**

Last Supper

Bible Verse: The Lord will protect you on your journeys—whether going or coming. (Psalm 121:8)

Bible Story: Matthew 26:17-30

Bible Background

Passover is a Jewish holiday that reflects on God's deliverance of the Hebrew people from slavery in Egypt. It is a celebration centered on remembering—every food they ate, every cup of wine was a way of remembering the time Moses, with God's help, liberated the Jewish people. Jesus and his friends made the trip to Jerusalem to celebrate. Jesus would have served as the head of the family group, saying the special blessings designated to the father. But Jesus had another message to deliver on this special evening. Jesus, as a good teacher, used two familiar items of Passover—the bread and the cup—to show what was about to happen to him and what these events would mean to the disciples.

As usual, the disciples did not understand what Jesus was trying to communicate. He would be leaving them. The days to come would be difficult for them. Jesus wanted them to have strength in one another and in the things they had done together. How sad it will be when one of Jesus' own friends will turn his back on these things and turn Jesus over to the guards. How sad it will be when Jesus' prediction of Peter's denial comes true. Jesus loves them anyway and shares this special meal with them all.

During the Lord's Supper, Jesus shared the bread and the cup with his friends and asked them to remember him. For younger children, it is important to use the celebration of Communion as a time of remembering Jesus and remembering that Jesus taught us to love and serve one another. As your children grow, so will their understanding of Communion and Jesus' love for us.

Devotion

Let's do lunch! We don't have to wait for Communion to remember Jesus. Each time you share a meal with someone, remember all the meals Jesus shared with his disciples and other followers. Fellowshipping with one another is one way we follow Jesus' teaching to love one another. It is difficult to dislike someone when you share a meal together.

BASIC

Plan

Bible Beginnings
Welcome
Picture the Bible Story
Bible Puzzle
Bible Play

Into the Bible
Time for the Bible Story
Open the Bible
Experience the Bible Story
Say the Bible Verse

Bible Connections
Bake Bread
Remember Relay

Live the Bible
Make a Bread Plate
Share Bread

Express Praise
Praise and Pray
Blessing

Bible Beginnings

Welcome

Supplies: Class Pack—p. 7, CD-ROM, CD player, tape, offering basket

- Display the Bible Verse Picture (Class Pack—p. 7) at eye level.
- Play, "The B-I-B-L-E" (CD-ROM), as you welcome each child.
- Show the children where to place their offerings on the worship table.

SAY: Today our Bible story is about a special meal Jesus ate with his friends.

- Point out the Bible Verse Picture, and say the Bible verse for the child.

Picture the Bible Story

Supplies: Leader Guide—p. 24, crayons or markers

- Photocopy "Jesus Shares a Special Meal" for each child.
- Give each child a copy of the picture.

SAY: Today our Bible story is about a special meal Jesus ate with his friends. Jesus and his friends ate bread together.

- Encourage each child to add bread to the empty plates and then decorate the whole picture with crayons or markers.

Bible Puzzle

Supplies: Bible Story Leaflet—Session 1, p. 4; crayons or markers

- Give each child a copy of "The Bread and the Cup."
- Encourage each child to use crayons or markers to make a stained glass window.

SAY: Today our Bible story is about a special meal Jesus ate with his friends. Jesus and his friends ate bread and drank wine together.

Bible Play

Supplies: unbreakable bowl or cutting board, rocks, birdseed or millet

SAY: In our Bible story, Jesus shared bread with his friends. In Bible times, people had to grind wheat or another kind of grain into flour so they could bake bread. Let's use a rock to grind grain, just like they did.

- Pour some birdseed or millet into an unbreakable bowl or onto a cutting board. Show the children how to use the rock to smash and grind the grain.

SAY: The meal Jesus shared with his friends was special, but the things they ate together were ordinary.

ASK: Do you eat bread? Do you drink juice?

SAY: Jesus wanted his friends to remember him often, so he used food items his friends would eat often to help them remember him.

Into the Bible

Time for the Bible Story

SAY: Let's pretend we are Jesus' friends going to see Jesus.

- Have the children line up behind you. Say the following action rhyme as you march around the room. End the poem in your story area.

SING: Let's go marching, marching, marching, all around the town.
Let's go marching, marching, marching, up the hills and down.
Let's go marching, marching, marching, 'cause marching is such fun.
Let's go marching, marching, marching to Jesus, God's own Son.

- Have the children sit down.

Open the Bible

Supplies: Bible Basics Storybook—pp. 160–161

- Tell the children the story, "Last Supper."

Experience the Bible Story

Supplies: CEB Bible; Bible Story Leaflet—Session 3, pp. 2–3

- Show the children the Bible.

TODAY'S BIBLE TOOL: The New Testament tells us about Jesus.

SAY: Our Bible is divided into two parts, the Old Testament and the New Testament. Stories about Jesus are in the New Testament.

- Show the children the beginning of the New Testament. Then show the children the Book of Matthew. Turn to the twenty-sixth chapter.

SAY: Our Bible story is about when Jesus shared a special meal with his friends. It's chapter twenty-six in the Book of Matthew. Listen as I tell the story. When I say the name, "Jesus," make the sign in American Sign Language for Jesus.

- Teach the children how to make the sign for Jesus (Leaflet, p. 2).

- Place the Leaflet in your Bible. Tell the children the story, "Last Supper" from the Bible Story Leaflet, and encourage them to do the sign as suggested.

SAY: Jesus wanted his friends to remember him.

ASK: What are some things you remember about Jesus?

Say the Bible Verse

Supplies: Class Pack—p. 7, Leader Guide—p. 93

- Show the children the Bible Verse Picture. Repeat the verse for the children.

- Teach the children signs from American Sign Language (Leader Guide) to go along with the verse.

- Encourage the children to make the signs as they say the verse again.

Bible Connections

Bake Bread

Supplies: canned biscuit dough, baking trays, flour, wax paper, hand-washing supplies, oven

SAY: Today our Bible story is about a special meal Jesus ate with his friends. Jesus and his friends ate bread and drank wine together. Let's bake bread to share together.

- Have the children wash their hands.
- Place a piece of wax paper on the table in front of each child.
- Give each child a piece of biscuit dough.

SAY: The bread Jesus and his friends ate at the special meal was called unleavened bread. That means the bread did not have yeast to make it fluffy. The bread was flat. Let's flatten our biscuits to be like unleavened bread.

- Show the children how to pat their biscuits flat. Let the children add a little flour to their hands if the biscuit dough sticks to their fingers.
- Place the flattened biscuits on a baking tray and bake according to the package directions. Plan to eat the bread later in the session.

Remember Relay

Supplies: none

- Have the children move to an open area of the room. Let the children line up on one side of the space.

SAY: Today our Bible story is about a special meal Jesus ate with his friends. Jesus and his friends ate bread and drank wine together at the special meal. We call this special meal Communion. We eat bread and drink juice together. It is one way we remember Jesus.

ASK: What do you remember about Jesus? *(Jesus loves us; God sent Jesus to teach us how to live; we celebrate Jesus' birthday at Christmas; Jesus welcomed the children; Jesus grew, just like we grow; we praise God for Jesus.)*

SAY: What good memories you have! Listen as I say a memory I have of Jesus. If you remember this, too, do what I tell you to do.
If you remember that we celebrate the birth of Jesus at Christmas, hop like a bunny across the room.
If you remember that magi followed a star to find a new king, clomp like a camel across the room.
If you remember that Jesus grew as we grow, gallop like a horse across the room.
If you remember that Jesus told the children to come to him, stomp like an elephant across the room.
If you remember that Jesus was baptized in a river, flap your wings like a dove and fly across the room.
If you remember that we can praise God for Jesus, jump like a kangaroo across the room.

- Have the children move back and forth across the room as you suggest.

Live the Bible

Make a Bread Plate

Supplies: clear plastic plates (two for each child), colored tissue paper, scissors, glue, glue brushes or paintbrushes, cups, water

- Cut colored tissue paper into small mosaic pieces.

SAY: Today our Bible story is about a special meal Jesus ate with his friends. Jesus and his friends ate bread and drank wine together. Let's make a bread plate to help us remember the special meal.

- Give each child one clear plastic plate. Show the children how to glue small pieces of colored tissue paper onto the center of the plate.
- Pour glue into a cup. Mix in a small amount of water.
- Have each child use a paintbrush to brush the glue mixture over all the paper.
- Give each child a second clear plastic plate. Help each child press the empty plate on top of the decorated plate to seal the tissue paper in the middle of the two plates.

Share Bread

Supplies: bread and bread plates made earlier

- Have the children sit down with their bread plates. Give each child a biscuit.

PRAY: Thank you, God, for bread to share. Thank you for Jesus. Amen.

TIP: If you chose not to make biscuits, purchase matzo crackers to share with the children. Be aware of any allergies.

Express Praise

Praise and Pray

Supplies: CD-ROM, CD player

- Sing with the children the song, "Hear Us As We Pray," from the CD-ROM.
- Encourage the children to name any prayer requests.

PRAY: Thank you, God, for all the wonderful things you have created. Amen.

Blessing

Supplies: none

- Have all the children face one side of the room.

SAY: If you journey this way, God is with you. *(Have the children turn to face the opposite side of the room.)* If you journey this way, God is with you.

- Call each child by name.

SAY: *(Child's name)*, God is always with you. *(Continue and bless each child.)*

Jesus Shares a Special Meal

The LORD **will protect you on your journeys—whether going or coming.
Psalm 121:8**

In the Garden

Bible Verse: The Lord will protect you on your journeys—whether going or coming. (Psalm 121:8)

Bible Story: Matthew 26:31-56

Bible Background

The story of Jesus' visit to the garden of Gethsemane to pray before his arrest and death is one that appears in all four Gospels. As is often the case, the story differs slightly in each account. Matthew and Mark say Jesus went to Gethsemane, and John says he went to a garden. Luke doesn't mention a garden or Gethsemane, but rather says that Jesus made his way to the Mount of Olives.

In the garden of Gethsemane, Jesus displays his humanness. We're told that Jesus knows his time of death is drawing near. When Jesus goes to the garden to pray, we see him sad and anxious as he contemplates the events to come. Jesus also wants human companionship. He takes Peter, James, and John with him as he goes farther into the garden. Jesus begs his closest friends to stay awake with him. The disciples failed in the task that Jesus gave them and instead of praying, they fell asleep. In Matthew and Mark, this scene repeats three times, with Jesus admonishing the disciples for falling asleep each time. Luke's account has the disciples only falling asleep once, and Luke appears to try to give the disciples an out by saying that they fell asleep because they were overcome with grief.

Devotion

There is something comforting in knowing the Son of God has experienced human emotions such as sadness and anxiety. Jesus knows how it feels. He gets it! Just as we can be comforted by these thoughts, we can also learn from Jesus' example in the way he responded to these emotions. Jesus prayed. We also can pray and receive comfort when we are sad and anxious.

You may want to add a prayer journal to your daily routine. This can be as simple as a spiral notebook or a book purchased specifically as a journal. Use the journal to write how you are feeling as you pray. Write down what you are praying for and note any answers that become apparent. End your daily journaling with gratitude. Make a list of at least three things you are grateful for each day.

BASIC

Plan

Bible Beginnings
- Welcome
- Picture the Bible Story
- Bible Puzzle
- Bible Play

Into the Bible
- Time for the Bible Story
- Open the Bible
- Experience the Bible Story
- Say the Bible Verse

Bible Connections
- Make a Garden
- Sleep, Sleep, Wake

Live the Bible
- Play Dough Feelings
- Pot a Prayer

Express Praise
- Praise and Pray
- Blessing

Bible Beginnings

Welcome

Supplies: Class Pack—Attendance Chart, p. 7; CD-ROM; CD player; tape; offering basket

- Display the Attendance Chart (Class Pack) and "Unit 1 Bible Verse Picture" (Class Pack—p. 7) at the children's eye level.
- Play, "The B-I-B-L-E" (CD-ROM), as you welcome each child.
- Show the children where to place their offerings on the worship table.

SAY: In our Bible story today, Jesus was feeling sad, so he went to a garden to pray.

- Point out the Bible Verse Picture, and say the Bible verse for the child.

Picture the Bible Story

Supplies: Leader Guide—p. 30, crayons or markers

- Photocopy "Jesus Prays" for each child. Give each child a copy of the picture.

SAY: In our Bible story today, Jesus was feeling sad, so he went to a garden to pray and talk to God.

- Encourage each child to decorate the picture with crayons or markers.

Bible Puzzle

Supplies: Bible Story Leaflet—Session 4, p. 4; crayons or markers

- Give each child a copy of "Find the Hidden Pictures" and encourage the children to find the hidden pictures.

SAY: In our Bible story today, Jesus was feeling sad, so he went to a garden to pray.

Bible Play

Supplies: green olives and black olives, olive oil, pictures of olive branches, stones, real or artificial wildflowers

- Provide items that will illustrate the things Jesus would have seen or touched in the garden of Gethsemane.

SAY: In our Bible story today, Jesus went to a garden to pray. The garden was an olive grove. That means there were trees that grew olives.

- Encourage the children to taste the olives. Pour a small amount of olive oil on each child's finger.
- Let the children examine the wildflowers.

Into the Bible

Time for the Bible Story

SAY: Let's pretend we are Jesus' friends going to see Jesus.

- Have the children line up behind you. Say the following action rhyme as you march around the room. End the poem in your story area.

SING: Let's go marching, marching, marching, all around the town.
Let's go marching, marching, marching, up the hills and down.
Let's go marching, marching, marching, 'cause marching is such fun.
Let's go marching, marching, marching to Jesus, God's own Son.

- Have the children sit down.

Open the Bible

Supplies: Bible Basics Storybook—pp. 162–163

- Tell the children the story, "In the Garden."

Experience the Bible Story

Supplies: CEB Bible; Bible Story Leaflet—Session 4, pp. 2–3

TODAY'S BIBLE TOOL: Stories about Jesus are in the New Testament.

SAY: Our Bible is divided into two parts, the Old Testament and the New Testament. Stories about Jesus are in the New Testament.

- Show the children the beginning of the New Testament. Then show the children the Book of Matthew. Turn to the twenty-sixth chapter.

SAY: Our Bible story is about when Jesus went to a garden to pray. It's chapter twenty-six in the Book of Matthew. Listen and watch as I tell the story.

- Place the Leaflet in your Bible. Tell the children the story, "In the Garden" from the Bible Story Leaflet, and encourage them to do the motions as suggested.

ASK: How do you think Jesus felt when he went to the garden to pray? How do you think Jesus felt when he finished praying?

Say the Bible Verse

Supplies: Class Pack—p. 7, Leader Guide—p. 93

- Show the children the Bible Verse Picture. Repeat the verse for the children.
- Teach the children signs from American Sign Language (Leader Guide) to go along with the verse.
- Encourage the children to make the signs as they say the verse again.

Bible Connections

Make a Garden

Supplies: mural paper, white coffee filters, crayons or markers, glue, tape

- Place a long piece of mural paper on the table or on the floor.

SAY: In our Bible story today, Jesus went to a garden to pray. He probably thought the garden was a peaceful place to be with God. Let's make a pretend garden. First, we will make flowers.

- Give each child a coffee filter to make a flower. Show the children how to flatten the filters out.

- Encourage each child to color the center of the coffee filter to be the center of the flower. Let each child make several flowers. Then have the children glue the flowers onto the mural paper.

- Let the children use crayons or markers to add grass, flower stems, and trees. Tape the mural on the floor or a wall in your story area. Have them sit around the mural.

SAY: Let's pretend we are in a beautiful garden. Everyone, sit quietly. Take a deep breath; now let it out slowly. Close your eyes and take another breath. Let's pray.

PRAY: Dear God, thank you for Jesus. Thank you for listening to us as we pray. Amen.

Sleep, Sleep, Wake

Supplies: none

- Have the children sit in a circle in an open area of the room for a game similar to "Duck, Duck, Goose."

SAY: Our Bible story is about what happened when Jesus went to a garden to pray. Jesus asked his friends to stay awake, but they went to sleep. Let's pretend we are friends of Jesus. We just can't stay awake. We are so sleepy. Let's go to sleep.

- Have the children pretend to sleep. Go around the circle, tapping each child's shoulder, saying, "Sleep." Then tap someone gently and say, "Wake up!" That child must jump up and walk quickly around the circle after you. Try to sit down in the empty space before the one who was awakened catches you.

- Play the game several times, changing who is the tapper.

Live the Bible

Play Dough Feelings

Supplies: play dough, paper, marker

- Draw a large happy-face circle on a paper for each child. Add the eyes, but do not draw a mouth. Give each child a copy of the face.

SAY: In our Bible story today, Jesus was feeling sad, so he went to a garden to pray. Let's make sad faces.

- Give each child a ball of play dough. Show the children how to pinch off a portion of the play dough and roll it into a "snake." Encourage the children to use the "snakes" to make frowns on their faces.

ASK: What do you do when you feel sad? One thing you can do when you feel sad is talk to God.

- Encourage the children to use the "snakes" to make smiles on their faces.

ASK: What do you do when you feel happy? One thing you can do when you feel happy is talk to God.

- Continue talking about feelings (mad, surprised, worried) and making the matching mouths out of play dough as the children show interest.

Pot a Prayer

Supplies: plastic or paper table covering, small paper cups or small terra cotta pots, stickers, plastic spoons, potting soil, grass seeds or marigold seeds, pitcher of water, craft sticks, markers

- Cover the work area with paper or plastic. Give each child a cup. Let the children decorate the cups with stickers. Help the children spoon potting soil into the cups.
- Sprinkle grass seeds or marigold seeds on top of the soil. Help the children cover the seeds lightly with more soil. Let the children sprinkle water over the seeds.
- Give each child a craft stick. Help them write something they would like to pray for on the craft sticks. Encourage the children to place their craft sticks inside their pots.

SAY: Our flowers can remind us of our Bible story today. Jesus went to a garden to pray. He probably thought the garden was a peaceful place to be with God.

Express Praise

Praise and Pray

Supplies: CD-ROM, CD player

- Sing with the children the song, "Hear Us As We Pray," from the CD-ROM.
- Encourage the children to name any prayer requests.

PRAY: Thank you, God, for all the wonderful things you have created. Amen.

Blessing

Supplies: none

- Have all the children face one side of the room.

SAY: If you journey this way, God is with you. *(Have the children turn to face the opposite side of the room.)* If you journey this way, God is with you.

- Call each child by name.

SAY: *(Child's name)*, God is always with you.

- Continue until you have blessed each child.

Jesus Prays

**The LORD will protect you on your journeys—whether going or coming.
Psalm 121:8**

Peter

Bible Verse: The Lord will protect you on your journeys—whether going or coming. (Psalm 121:8)

Bible Story: Matthew 26:57-58, 69-75

Bible Background

When Jesus called Peter to be his disciple, Peter warned him that he was a sinful man (Luke 5:8). Jesus called Peter to follow him anyway, saying, "Don't be afraid. From now on, you will be fishing for people" (Luke 5:10).

Last week when we heard the story of Jesus praying in the garden, we heard Jesus tell Peter that Peter would deny Jesus three times before the rooster crowed. Although Peter was determined to prove Jesus wrong, he did not.

Unlike Judas, whose betrayal of Jesus was planned, Peter did not set out to deny Jesus; it just happened. Peter was trying to follow Jesus. After Jesus was arrested, Peter followed along at a distance. As he sat around a fire in the courtyard, the accusations began to come: "You were also with Jesus, the Galilean"; "This man was with Jesus, the man from Nazareth"; "You must be one of them."

Put yourself in Peter's place. The Roman soldiers have arrested Jesus, and things are starting to get ugly. Peter was scared. He may have feared his life was in danger, and it might have been. When the accusations began, Peter acted out of self-preservation. He denied his association with Jesus. And then he heard the rooster. When the cock crowed, Peter remembered Jesus' words. Peter had failed Jesus, even before Jesus' trial had begun. Peter cried.

Peter did redeem himself. After the Resurrection, Peter became one of Jesus' most enthusiastic evangelists, spreading the good news far and wide.

Devotion

It can be helpful to remember Peter's fear. All too often, we see the followers of Jesus as some sort of superhumans, and we think we can never be like them. But Peter and all the rest were very human—they had the same doubts and fears we encounter. Because he was afraid, Peter denied he knew Jesus. Sometimes we don't do what is right because we are afraid. The good news is that just as Peter was given another chance, so are we. Jesus never denies us.

BASIC

Plan

Bible Beginnings
Welcome
Picture the Bible Story
Bible Puzzle
Bible Play

Into the Bible
Time for the Bible Story
Open the Bible
Experience the Bible Story
Say the Bible Verse

Bible Connections
Peter's Rooster
Peter Heard the Rooster Crow

Live the Bible
How Do You Feel?
Review and Crow

Express Praise
Praise and Pray
Blessing

Bible Beginnings

Welcome

Supplies: Class Pack—Attendance Chart, p. 7; CD-ROM; CD player; tape; offering basket

- Display the Attendance Chart (Class Pack) and "Unit 1 Bible Verse Picture" (Class Pack—p. 7) at the children's eye level.
- Play, "The B-I-B-L-E" (CD-ROM), as you welcome each child.
- Show the children where to place their offerings on the worship table.

SAY: Our Bible story today is about Peter, a friend of Jesus. Peter said Jesus was not his friend, and then Peter heard a rooster crow.

- Point out the Bible Verse Picture, and say the Bible verse for the child.

Picture the Bible Story

Supplies: Leader Guide—p. 36, crayons or markers

- Photocopy "Peter" for each child.
- Give each child a copy of the picture.

SAY: Our Bible story today is about the time when Peter was sitting with other people around a fire, and he said Jesus was not his friend.

- Encourage each child to decorate the picture with crayons or markers.

Bible Puzzle

Supplies: Bible Story Leaflet—Session 5, p. 4; crayons or markers

- Give each child a copy of "Rooster Dot-to-Dot."
- Encourage the children to connect the dots to draw the rooster.

SAY: A rooster is important in today's Bible story. After Peter said Jesus was not his friend, Peter heard a rooster crow. Hearing the crow made Peter very sad. He was sorry he said that he didn't know Jesus.

Bible Play

Supplies: play dough, craft sticks

SAY: A rooster is important in today's Bible story. After Peter said Jesus was not his friend, Peter heard a rooster crow. Let's make roosters out of play dough.

- Give each child a lump of play dough. Encourage the children to form the dough into a ball.
- Give each child several craft sticks. Show each child how to stick the craft sticks into the ball to make the rooster's tail.

SAY: Hearing the crow made Peter very sad. He was sorry he said that he didn't know Jesus.

Into the Bible

Time for the Bible Story

SAY: Let's pretend we are Jesus' friends going to see Jesus.

- Have the children line up behind you. Say the following action rhyme as you march around the room. End the poem in your story area.

SING: Let's go marching, marching, marching, all around the town.
Let's go marching, marching, marching, up the hills and down.
Let's go marching, marching, marching, 'cause marching is such fun.
Let's go marching, marching, marching to Jesus, God's own Son.

- Have the children sit down.

Open the Bible

Supplies: Bible Basics Storybook—pp. 164-165

- Tell the children the story, "Peter."

Experience the Bible Story

Supplies: CEB Bible; Bible Story Leaflet—Session 5, pp. 2-3

- Show the children the Bible.

TODAY'S BIBLE TOOL: Stories about Jesus are in the New Testament.

SAY: Our Bible is divided into two parts, the Old Testament and the New Testament. Stories about Jesus are in the New Testament.

- Show the children the beginning of the New Testament. Then show the children the Book of Matthew. Turn to the twenty-sixth chapter.

SAY: Our Bible story is when Peter denied knowing Jesus. It's chapter twenty-six in the Book of Matthew. Listen and watch as I tell the story.

- Place the Leaflet in your Bible. Tell the children the story, "Peter" from the Bible Story Leaflet, and encourage them to do the motions as suggested.

ASK: How do you think Peter felt when he heard the rooster crow?

SAY: Peter made a bad choice when he said he didn't know Jesus. But this was not the end of Peter and Jesus' friendship. Jesus still loved Peter.

Say the Bible Verse

Supplies: Class Pack—p. 7, Leader Guide—p. 93

- Show the children the Bible Verse Picture. Repeat the verse for the children.
- Teach the children signs from American Sign Language (Leader Guide) to go along with the verse.
- Encourage the children to make the signs as they say the verse again.

Bible Connections

Peter's Rooster

Supplies: red paper plates or inexpensive white paper plates and small pieces of red tissue paper, yellow construction paper, craft feathers, googly eyes, scissors, glue, crayons or markers

- Cut a three- to four-inch square from yellow construction paper for each child.

SAY: A rooster crowed after the third time Peter said Jesus was not his friend. Even though Peter made a bad choice, he was not bad, and Jesus forgave him. The rooster can help us remember that Jesus loves us, no matter what.

- Give each child a paper plate. If you have white plates, let the children glue on red tissue paper. Encourage each child to cover the entire plate with the red paper.

- Give each child a square of the yellow construction paper. Show the children how to fold the square in half to make a triangle.

- Help each child glue the triangle onto the center of the paper plate to make the rooster's beak. Give each child a pair of googly eyes. Let each child glue the eyes to the paper plate above the beak.

- Give each child three or more craft feathers. Encourage the children to glue at least one feather at the top of the paper plate to make the rooster's comb. Let the children glue the other feathers wherever they wish on their roosters.

Peter Heard the Rooster Crow

Supplies: rooster faces made earlier

- Have the children hold their rooster faces and sit down.

SAY: Let's sing a song to help us remember today's story. At the very end of the song, hold up your rooster face and say, "Cock-a-doodle-doo!"

- Sing the song printed below to the tune of "The Muffin Man."

SING: Peter, do you know this man, know this man, know this man?
Peter, do you know this man? He is your friend.
No, I do not know this man, know this man, know this man.
No, I do not know this man. He's not my friend.
Peter heard the rooster crow, rooster crow, rooster crow.
Peter heard the rooster crow. Cock-a-doodle-doo!

Live the Bible

How Do You Feel?

Supplies: CD-ROM, CD player, construction paper, tape, marker

- Draw a question mark on a piece of construction paper.

- Tape construction paper on the floor in a circle for a game similar to a cake walk. Have one paper for each child. Include the question mark in the circle.

SAY: Peter felt afraid, and then he felt sad. We all have lots of feelings. Let's play a game about feelings. Walk around the circle while the music plays. When the music stops, stop walking. If you stopped on the question mark, go to the center of the circle.

- Play the music (CD-ROM) and start walking. Stop the music. Have the child who stopped on the question mark move to the center of the circle.

SAY: Show me how you feel. *(sad, happy, afraid, mad)*

- Let the remaining children guess how the child in the center is feeling. Have the child move back into the circle and continue the game.

Review and Crow

Supplies: rooster faces made earlier

- Have the children hold their rooster faces and sit on the floor.

SAY: Let's remember some of the stories we've learned about Jesus. Listen to what I say. If what I say is true, jump up, hold up your rooster face, and crow as loud as you can, then sit back down. If what I say is not true, stay seated.

SAY: Jesus helped a man by healing his hand. *(Crow.)*
Jesus told his friends to get rid of the children. *(Stay seated.)*
Jesus wanted the children to come to him. *(Crow.)*
Jesus ate bread at a special meal with his friends. *(Crow.)*
Jesus asked his friends to order pizza. *(Stay seated.)*
Jesus went to a garden to pray. *(Crow.)*
Three of Jesus' friends kept falling asleep while Jesus prayed. *(Crow.)*
Peter cried when he heard the rooster crow. *(Crow.)*

Express Praise

Praise and Pray

Supplies: CD-ROM, CD player

- Sing with the children the song, "Hear Us As We Pray," from the CD-ROM. Encourage the children to name any prayer requests.

PRAY: Thank you, God, for our friend, Jesus. Amen.

Blessing

Supplies: none

- Have all the children face one side of the room.

SAY: If you journey this way, God is with you. *(Have the children turn to face the opposite side of the room.)* If you journey this way, God is with you.

- Call each child by name.

SAY: *(Child's name)*, God is always with you.

- Continue until you have blessed each child.

Peter

**The LORD will protect you on your journeys—whether going or coming.
Psalm 121:8**

Hosanna!

Bible Verse: Now hurry, go and tell his disciples, "He's been raised from the dead." (Matthew 28:7)

Bible Story: Matthew 21:1-11; 27:32-66

Bible Background

Each year many of us celebrate the Sunday before Easter by waving palm branches and shouting, "Hosanna!" This story is one that is found in all four Gospels. In Matthew's account, the palm branches were laid on the road rather than waved in the air. People also lined the road with clothes for the animal that Jesus was riding to walk on. The story in Matthew also mentions both a donkey and a colt, and it is unclear from the wording which animal Jesus was riding.

The celebration that occurred when Jesus entered Jerusalem was similar to the reception of military leaders returning victorious from battle. It is probable that some in the crowd expected Jesus to be a military ruler who would free them from the Roman emperor. Because we know the rest of the story, we are aware Jesus was leader of a quite different kingdom. Jesus came as a peaceful leader to teach people to love and serve one another. Jesus entered Jerusalem riding humbly on a donkey rather than pompously on a warhorse.

Palm Sunday marks the beginning of Holy Week. This Sunday is also known as Passion Sunday, reminding us that in just a few short days, the cries of "Hosanna!" changed to "Crucify him!" and Jesus was led to the cross. The details of Jesus' crucifixion are missing from today's lesson. We want children to understand that Jesus was put to death not because he was a bad person, but because people did not understand what his message was all about. We want them to know the story, but we don't want to distract children with details that focus on the blood and violence of Jesus' death. It's important the children hear that Jesus' death and burial is not the end of the story.

Devotion

Today's lesson sends us on a roller coaster of emotions. Remembering Jesus with palms and shouts of praise is exciting. Then remembering the other events of Holy Week bring us great sadness. Thankfully, we know Jesus' death is not the end of the story. We can move forward through this week anticipating the joy of the Resurrection.

BASIC

Plan

Bible Beginnings
Welcome
Picture the Bible Story
Bible Puzzle
Bible Play

Into the Bible
Time for the Bible Story
Open the Bible
Experience the Bible Story
Say the Bible Verse

Bible Connections
Paper Palms
Paper Robes

Live the Bible
Palm Sunday Parade
Not the End of the Story

Express Praise
Praise and Pray
Blessing

Bible Beginnings

Welcome

Supplies: Class Pack—Attendance Chart, p. 8; CD-ROM; CD player; tape; offering basket

• Display the Attendance Chart (Class Pack) and "Unit 2 Bible Verse Picture" (Class Pack—p. 8) at the children's eye level.

• Play, "The B-I-B-L-E" (CD-ROM), as you welcome each child.

• Show the children where to place their offerings on the worship table.

SAY: Today is Palm Sunday. Our Bible story is about a time when Jesus rode a donkey into the city.

• Point out the Bible Verse Picture, and say the Bible verse for the child.

Picture the Bible Story

Supplies: Leader Guide—p. 42, crayons or markers

• Photocopy "Hosanna!" for each child. Give each child a copy of the picture.

SAY: Today our Bible story is about a time when Jesus rode a donkey into the city. The people were happy to see Jesus. They cut palm branches and laid them on the ground for the donkey to walk on. They shouted, "Hosanna!"

• Encourage the children to decorate the picture with crayons or markers.

Bible Puzzle

Supplies: Bible Story Leaflet—Session 6, p. 4; crayons or markers

• Give each child a copy of "Floating Letters."

• Let the children follow the directions to complete the puzzle.

SAY: In our Bible story today, Jesus rides a donkey into the city. The people were happy to see Jesus. They shouted, "Hosanna!" as Jesus rode by.

Bible Play

Supplies: real palm branches or other green leaves, mallets, plain paper, tape

SAY: Our Bible story is about the time Jesus rode a donkey into the city. The people cut palm branches and laid them on the road for the donkey to walk on.

• Tape a piece of paper to a hard surface like a tabletop or the floor. Place a palm branch on top of the paper.

• Show the children how to use the mallet to pound on top of the palm branch.

• Lift the palm branch. The green from the branch will stick to the paper.

SAY: The green on the paper is from the palm branch. It is called chlorophyll. Chlorophyll is what makes the branch green.

• Give each child an opportunity to pound a palm branch.

Into the Bible

Time for the Bible Story

- Sing the song, "The Children Sang," as you lead the children to your story area. The song is sung to the tune of "The Muffin Man."

SING: "Hosanna," the children sang, the children sang, the children sang. "Hosanna," the children sang. Hosanna!

- Have the children sit down.

SAY: When the people saw Jesus riding into the city, they shouted, "Hosanna!"

Open the Bible

Supplies: Bible Basics Storybook—pp. 158–159, 166–167

- Tell the children the stories, "Hosanna!" and "Jesus' Crucifixion."

Experience the Bible Story

Supplies: CEB Bible; Bible Story Leaflet—Session 6, pp. 2–3

- Show the children the Bible.

TODAY'S BIBLE TOOL: Stories about Jesus are in the New Testament.

SAY: Our Bible is divided into two parts, the Old Testament and the New Testament. Stories about Jesus are in the New Testament.

- Show the children the beginning of the New Testament. Then show the children the Book of Matthew. Turn to the twenty-first chapter.

SAY: We have two Bible stories today. The first Bible story is about Jesus riding a donkey into the city. It's chapter twenty-one in the Book of Matthew. For this story, you need to learn the sign for "hosanna" in American Sign Language.

- Teach the children the sign for "hosanna" (Leaflet, p. 2).

SAY: Our second story is about Jesus' death. It's chapter twenty-seven in the Book of Matthew. Listen and watch as I tell both stories.

- Place the Leaflet in your Bible. Tell the children the story, "Hosanna!" from the Bible Story Leaflet, and encourage them to do the sign and motions as suggested.

SAY: That's the end of our Bible stories for today, but it's not the end of Jesus' story. Next week we'll celebrate that Jesus did not stay in the tomb. Jesus is alive!

Say the Bible Verse

Supplies: Class Pack—p. 8, Leader Guide—p. 94

- Show the children the Bible Verse Picture. Repeat the verse for the children.
- Teach the children signs from American Sign Language (Leader Guide) to go along with the verse.
- Encourage the children to make the signs as they say the verse again.

Bible Connections

Paper Palms

Supplies: safety scissors, green construction paper, craft sticks, tape, marker

SAY: Today is the day we remember the Bible story of Jesus riding a donkey into the city. Many, many people were happy to see Jesus. Some people cut palm branches from palm trees and laid the branches on the ground in front of the donkey. The donkey walked over the branches as Jesus rode into the city. Let's make paper palm branches using the palms of our hands.

- Give each child a piece of green construction paper. Show each child how to place one hand on the paper with the fingers spread wide. Trace around the hand.
- Let the children use safety scissors to cut out their handprint. Younger children may need help cutting.
- Encourage each child to make three or more handprints.
- Help each child tape her or his handprints onto a craft stick to make a palm branch.

Paper Robes

Supplies: large pieces of newsprint, scissors, fabric scraps, glue, crayons or markers

SAY: Today is the special day we remember the Bible story of Jesus riding a donkey into the city. Many, many people wanted to show everyone in the city that Jesus was special. Some people took off their robes and laid them on the ground. The donkey walked over the robes as Jesus rode into the city. Let's make paper robes.

- Prepare a robe for each child. Fold a large piece of newsprint in half. Cut an oval across the fold to make a hole for the child's head.
- Let the children decorate the folded and cut newsprint with crayons or markers and by gluing on small pieces of fabric scraps.
- Help each child put the paper robe over his or her head and wear it like a poncho.

Live the Bible

Palm Sunday Parade

Supplies: paper palms and paper robes made earlier, shirts or pieces of fabric

SAY: Today is the special day we remember the Bible story of Jesus riding a donkey into the city. Many, many people were happy to see Jesus. They wanted to show everyone in the city that Jesus was special. They cut palm branches from palm trees and laid the branches on the ground in front of the donkey. They also took off their robes and laid them on the ground. The donkey walked over the branches and robes as Jesus rode into the city.

- Choose a child to be "Jesus."

- Have the remaining children be the crowd who welcomed Jesus. Let each child hold either a paper palm or a shirt and line up in two facing lines in an open area of the room or in a hallway.
- Have "Jesus" walk down the center of the two lines. Let the "crowd" lay their paper palms and shirts down on the floor for "Jesus" to walk on.
- Encourage everyone to shout, "Hosanna!" several times.

Not the End of the Story

Supplies: painters' tape, plain paper, watercolor paints and brushes, containers of water, paper or plastic table covering

- Cover the table with paper or plastic.
- Use the painters' tape to make a cross in the center of a piece of plain paper for each child.
- Set out watercolors, containers of water, and brushes for the children to share.
- Give each child a piece of paper with a tape cross.
- Encourage the children to use the watercolor paints to paint completely over their papers. They can also paint over the tape cross.
- When the paint is dry, gently remove the masking tape to reveal the cross shape.

SAY: A cross reminds us of how Jesus died. But Jesus' death is not the end of the story. Jesus did not stay on the cross or in the tomb. God made Jesus alive again. On Easter, we'll celebrate that Jesus lives!

Express Praise

Praise and Pray

Supplies: CD-ROM, CD player

- Sing with the children the song, "Hear Us As We Pray," from the CD-ROM.
- Encourage the children to name any prayer requests.

PRAY: Thank you, God, for Jesus. Amen.

Blessing

Supplies: lip balm or olive oil

- Have the children stand in a circle.
- Go to each child and use the lip balm to draw a cross on the back of the child's hand. You can also dip your finger in a small amount of olive oil and use the oil to draw a cross.

SAY: Jesus is not on the cross or in the tomb. Jesus is alive. Jesus loves *(child's name)*.

- Continue until you have blessed each child.

Hosanna!

Now hurry, go and tell his disciples, "He's been raised from the dead."
Matthew 28:7

Easter

Bible Verse: Now hurry, go and tell his disciples, "He's been raised from the dead." (Matthew 28:7)

Bible Story: Matthew 28:1-10

Bible Background

The Christian church has chosen to gather on Sunday mornings to remind ourselves of that early Sunday morning many years ago when it was discovered that the tomb was empty. Every Sunday morning is a "little Easter" celebration. We come together to praise God and give thanks for the good news of the empty tomb.

Although their accounts differ in details, Matthew, Mark, Luke, and John all give an account of the empty tomb. In Matthew's account of the empty tomb, it is Mary Magdalene and the other Mary who make the discovery. The angel then tells them to go and tell the disciples.

On the way to do just that, the women meet Jesus himself. Jesus also tells the women to go and tell the disciples he is alive, but with an important choice of words. Jesus says, "Go and tell my brothers that I am going into Galilee. They will see me there." In the events preceding Jesus' resurrection, all of the disciples left Jesus and ran away, except for Peter—who denied Jesus three times—and Judas—who betrayed Jesus and then killed himself. We can assume the disciples were experiencing feelings of guilt and anxiety. In referring to the disciples as brothers, Jesus indicates they are still part of his family.

Easter is the highlight of the Christian Year, a day of great celebration. Jesus is alive! It is time to celebrate new life in all its forms. Children may, at Easter, have a great number of questions about the Resurrection. Answer their questions as simply and as honestly as possible. As adults, we still don't have all the answers. It is perfectly acceptable to say, "I don't know." What we do know is that with God, all things are possible.

Devotion

Enjoy celebrating Easter with the children in your class, with your church family at church, and your family at home. Easter is a time to look at all the signs of new life we see in God's world—eggs that hatch into baby birds, caterpillars that change into butterflies, and flowers that bloom in the spring. It is a time to celebrate God's great, never-ending love. Jesus is alive!

BASIC

Plan

Bible Beginnings
- Welcome
- Picture the Bible Story
- Bible Puzzle
- Bible Play

Into the Bible
- Time for the Bible Story
- Open the Bible
- Experience the Bible Story
- Say the Bible Verse

Bible Connections
- Egg Roll
- The Empty Tomb

Live the Bible
- Make Paper Lilies
- This Special Day

Express Praise
- Praise and Pray
- Blessing

Bible Beginnings

Welcome

Supplies: Class Pack—p. 8, CD-ROM, CD player, tape, offering basket

• Display the Unit 2 Bible Verse Picture (Class Pack—p. 8) at eye level.

• Play, "The B-I-B-L-E" (CD-ROM), as you welcome each child.

• Show the children where to place their offerings on the worship table.

SAY: Today is Easter! It's a special day to remember that Jesus is alive.

• Point out the Bible Verse Picture, and say the Bible verse for the child.

Picture the Bible Story

Supplies: Leader Guide—p. 48, crayons or markers

• Photocopy "Jesus Lives!" for each child.

• Give each child a copy of the picture.

SAY: Jesus died and was placed in a tomb. A tomb is a place where people are buried. Look at your picture. Where is Jesus? He's not in the tomb; he is alive!

• Encourage the children to decorate the picture with crayons or markers.

Bible Puzzle

Supplies: Bible Story Leaflet—Session 7, p. 4; crayons or markers

• Give each child a copy of "Trace the Words."

• Let the children trace the words to discover what the women learned about Jesus.

SAY: Today is Easter! It's a special day to remember that Jesus is alive.

Bible Play

Supplies: plastic Easter eggs (one for each child), spring stickers (flowers, butterflies, chicks, and so forth)

• Place a sticker in every Easter egg, except one. Leave this egg empty, but save the extra sticker.

• Have the children cover their eyes with their hands.

• Quickly hide the Easter eggs around the room.

SAY: Open your eyes. Each of you, look for one Easter egg. When you've found one egg, come back and sit down in our story area.

• Have the children hunt for the eggs.

• After all the children are sitting down, have the children open their eggs.

ASK: What's in your egg? *(All but one child will say a sticker.)*

SAY: Easter eggs help us remember new life. Eggs hatch, and a new life is born.

ASK: Did someone get an empty egg?

SAY: The empty egg can also remind us of new life. On the first Easter morning, two women went to the tomb where Jesus was buried, but the tomb was empty.

ASK: Why was the tomb empty? *(Because Jesus is alive!)*

- Give the child with the empty egg the extra sticker.

Into the Bible

Time for the Bible Story

- Have the children stay seated in your story area.

SAY: Today is Easter! It's a special day to remember that Jesus is alive.

- Sing the following song to the tune of "The Farmer in the Dell."

SING: Oh, we remember Jesus.
Oh, we remember Jesus.
On this happy Easter day,
oh, we remember Jesus.

Oh, Jesus is alive,
Oh, Jesus is alive.
On this happy Easter day,
oh, Jesus is alive.

Open the Bible

Supplies: Bible Basics Storybook—pp. 168–169

- Tell the children the story, "Easter."

Experience the Bible Story

Supplies: CEB Bible; Bible Story Leaflet—Session 7, pp. 2–3

- Show the children the Bible.

TODAY'S BIBLE TOOL: Stories about Jesus are in the New Testament.

SAY: Our Bible is divided into two parts, the Old Testament and the New Testament. Stories about Jesus are in the New Testament.

- Show the children the beginning of the New Testament. Then show the children the Book of Matthew. Turn to the twenty-eighth chapter.

SAY: Our Bible story is about what happened on the first Easter morning. It's chapter twenty-eight in the Book of Matthew.

- Place the Leaflet in your Bible. Tell the children the story, "Easter" from the Bible Story Leaflet, and encourage them to do the motions as suggested.

Say the Bible Verse

Supplies: Class Pack—p. 8, Leader Guide—p. 94

- Show the children the Bible Verse Picture. Repeat the verse for the children.
- Teach the children signs from American Sign Language (Leader Guide) to go along with the verse.
- Encourage the children to make the signs as they say the verse again.

Bible Connections

Egg Roll

Supplies: plastic Easter eggs, masking tape

- Have the children move to one side of the room. Use masking tape to mark a starting line in front of the children. Mark a finish line on the opposite side of the room. Make sure the area between the lines is clear.
- Give each child a plastic Easter egg.

SAY: Here is an empty Easter egg. The empty eggs remind us of the empty tomb.

- Explain to the children that the object of the game is to roll the Easter eggs to the finish line. Let the children use their hands to roll the eggs.
- Begin the game by saying, "Go!"

The Empty Tomb

Supplies: play dough or air-drying clay, Easter eggs, paper plates, green construction paper scraps, glue

SAY: On the first Easter morning, two women went to the tomb where Jesus was buried. The women discovered that the tomb was empty. Let's use play dough *(or clay)* to make an empty tomb.

- Give each child a paper plate. Have the children turn the paper plates upside down.
- Give the children green construction paper scraps. Show the children how to tear the paper into smaller strips.
- Encourage the children to glue the green strips onto the bottom of the paper plate to make grass. Set the plates aside.
- Give each child a portion of dough or clay and one half of a plastic Easter egg.
- Show the children how to mold the play dough or clay around the outside of the plastic egg so that the egg becomes the base for the tomb.
- Have the children press one side of the dough or clay tomb onto the paper plate so the inside of the egg faces out.

Live the Bible

Make Paper Lilies

Supplies: white construction paper, crayons or markers, safety scissors, yellow and green chenille stems, tape

- Cut yellow chenille stems into three-inch pieces. Each child will need one piece.
- Help each child trace a hand, with fingers spread, on white construction paper. Let the children cut out their handprints. Younger children may need help cutting.
- Give each child a yellow chenille piece and a green chenille stem. Help each child make a *U* shape with the yellow stem. Wrap one end of the green stem around the

bottom of the *U*. Curl the ends of the *U* to make the center of the lily. Have the child tape the stem and center to the palm of the hand cutout.

- Help each child roll the paper lengthwise, wrap it around the chenille stem, and tape it closed.
- Encourage each child to curl the fingers outward to look like lily petals.

SAY: Today is Easter, a special day to celebrate that Jesus is alive! Many churches add lilies to the sanctuary to decorate for Easter. The lily reminds us that Jesus is alive.

This Special Day

Supplies: none

SAY: Today is a special day to remember that Jesus is alive! It's a day to be happy. Let's sing a song *(tune: The Wheels on the Bus)* that shows how we feel about Easter.

SING: On this Easter day, let's clap our hands, *(Clap hands.)*
clap our hands, clap our hands.
On this Easter day let's clap our hands for Jesus lives.

On this Easter day, let's stomp our feet, *(Stomp feet.)*
stomp our feet, stomp our feet.
On this Easter day let's stomp our feet for Jesus lives.

On this Easter day, let's turn around, *(Turn around.)*
turn around, turn around.

On this Easter day, let's turn around for Jesus lives.

On this Easter day, let's jump for joy, *(Jump in place.)*
jump for joy, jump for joy.
On this Easter day, let's jump for joy for Jesus lives.

On this Easter day, let's shout, "Hooray!" *(Shout, "Hooray.")*
shout, "Hooray! shout, "Hooray!"
On this Easter day, let's shout, "Hooray!" for Jesus lives.

Express Praise

Praise and Pray

Supplies: CD-ROM, CD player

- Sing with the children the song, "Hear Us As We Pray," from the CD-ROM.
- Encourage the children to name any prayer requests.

PRAY: Thank you, God, for Easter. We know he is alive! Amen.

Blessing

Supplies: lip balm or olive oil

- Have the children stand in a circle.
- Go to each child and use lip balm to draw a cross on the back of the child's hand. You can also dip your finger in a small amount of olive oil and use it to draw a cross.

SAY: Jesus is not on the cross or in the tomb. Jesus is alive. Jesus loves *(child's name)*.

- Continue until you have blessed each child.

Jesus Lives!

**Now hurry, go and tell his disciples, "He's been raised from the dead."
(Matthew 28:7)**

Breakfast on the Beach

Bible Verse: Now hurry, go and tell his disciples, "He's been raised from the dead. (Matthew 28:7)

Bible Story: John 21:1-19

Bible Background

Our Bible story today is a post-Resurrection appearance of Jesus. This appearance story also contains elements of a miracle story. The disciples have been fishing all night, but have not caught anything. In the morning, they see Jesus on the shore, though they don't recognize him at first. Jesus tells them to let their net down on the other side of the boat. This story is similar to the one found in Luke 5 when Jesus calls Simon Peter, James, and John to follow him and be his disciples. When Jesus' instructions are followed, the result is a miraculous catch of fish—153 fish, in fact. Biblical scholars have wondered why John included the exact number of fish caught. Theories range from suggestions of a mathematical significance to the number 153, to the explanation that an eyewitness counted the number of fish caught. Regardless of the reason for the specific number, the message is that Jesus didn't just provide fish; Jesus provided more than enough.

Jesus cooks the disciples a breakfast of bread and fish. This meal is a reminder of the miraculous feeding of the five thousand with bread and fish. It is also reminiscent of Jesus' last meal with the disciples before his death, when they shared the Passover meal and Jesus broke the bread.

At this point, the story turns into a conversation between Jesus and Peter. Jesus asks Peter if Peter loves him. In fact, Jesus asks Peter this question three times. Before Jesus' death, Peter denied Jesus three times. Now Jesus gives Peter three opportunities to profess his love for Jesus. And when Peter assures Jesus of his love, Jesus gives him directions for the future: "Feed my sheep." During his ministry, Jesus referred to himself as the Good Shepherd who cared for his flock—that would be us. Jesus is turning over the care of his flock to Peter. "The way to show your love for me," Jesus tells Peter, "is to take care of those I love."

Devotion

Jesus' instructions to Peter are true for us today as well. The best way to show our love for Jesus is by taking care of those he loves. As a teacher, you show your love for Jesus by taking care of the children in your class.

What are other ways you show love?

BASIC

Plan

Bible Beginnings
- Welcome
- Picture the Bible Story
- Bible Puzzle
- Bible Play

Into the Bible
- Time for the Bible Story
- Open the Bible
- Experience the Bible Story
- Say the Bible Verse

Bible Connections
- Net Fishing
- Fish in the Sea

Live the Bible
- Heart Stamps
- Play Dough Hearts

Express Praise
- Praise and Pray
- Blessing

Bible Beginnings

Welcome

Supplies: Class Pack—p. 8, CD-ROM, CD player, tape, offering basket

• Display the Bible Verse Picture (Class Pack—p. 8) at eye level.

• Play, "The B-I-B-L-E" (CD-ROM), as you welcome each child.

• Show the children where to place their offerings on the worship table.

SAY: Today our Bible story is about a time when Jesus and his friends had breakfast together on the beach.

• Point out the Bible Verse Picture, and say the Bible verse for the child.

Picture the Bible Story

Supplies: Leader Guide—p. 54, crayons or markers

• Photocopy "Breakfast on the Beach" for each child.

• Give each child a copy of the picture.

SAY: Today our Bible story is about a time when Jesus and his friends had breakfast together on the beach. They ate bread and fish.

• Encourage the children to decorate the picture with crayons or markers.

Bible Puzzle

Supplies: Bible Story Leaflet—Session 8, p. 4; crayons or markers

• Give each child a copy of "What's for Breakfast?"

• Have the children follow the directions to complete the page.

SAY: Jesus and his friends ate bread and fish for breakfast.

Bible Play

Supplies: construction paper, scissors, crayons or markers, stapler and staples

• Cut construction paper into about 3-by-8 strips. Each child will need one strip.

• Fold each strip in half, bringing the short sides together. Then cut a small triangle out of the center of the folded end.

SAY: Today our Bible story is about a time when Jesus and his friends had breakfast together on the beach. But before they had breakfast, Jesus' friends went fishing and caught fish to eat.

• Give each child a folded strip and a triangle. Help each child staple the triangle on the opposite end of the strip from the fold. The triangle will make the tail of the fish.

• Let the children use crayons or markers to add eyes and colorful scales to the paper fish.

SAY: We'll use our fish when we hear the Bible story.

Into the Bible

Time for the Bible Story

- Have the children follow you to your story area. Sing the song printed below to the tune of "The Farmer in the Dell."

SING: Oh, we remember Jesus.
Oh, we remember Jesus.
On this happy Easter day,
oh, we remember Jesus.

Oh, Jesus is alive,
Oh, Jesus is alive.
On this happy Easter day,
oh, Jesus is alive.

Open the Bible

Supplies: Bible Basics Storybook—pp. 256-259

- Tell the children the stories, "Come to Breakfast!" and "Feed My Sheep."

Experience the Bible Story

Supplies: CEB Bible; Bible Story Leaflet—Session 8, pp. 2-3; story fish made earlier

- Show the children the Bible.

TODAY'S BIBLE TOOL: Stories about Jesus are in the New Testament.

SAY: Our Bible is divided into two parts, the Old Testament and the New Testament. Stories about Jesus are in the New Testament.

- Show the children the beginning of the New Testament. Then show the children the Book of John. Turn to the twenty-first chapter.

SAY: Our Bible story is about what happened when Jesus and his friends had breakfast on the beach. It's chapter twenty-one in the Book of John.

- Give the children the paper fish made earlier. Have the children hold the fish as you tell the story.

- Place the Leaflet in your Bible. Tell the children the story, "Breakfast on the Beach" from the Bible Story Leaflet, and encourage them to throw their fish into the air as suggested.

ASK: How do you think Jesus' friends felt when they saw Jesus on the shore? How do you think Peter felt when Jesus asked him if Peter loved him three times? What do you think Jesus meant when he told Peter to feed my sheep?

Say the Bible Verse

Supplies: Class Pack—p. 8, Leader Guide—p. 94

- Show the children the Bible Verse Picture. Repeat the verse for the children.

- Teach the children signs from American Sign Language (Leader Guide) to go along with the verse.

- Encourage the children to make the signs as they say the verse again.

Bible Connections

Net Fishing

Supplies: paper fish made earlier; glue; blue construction paper; crayons with papers removed; scissors; netting, netted bath poufs, or woven fruit bags; tape

- Cut netting fabric into 8-by-10 rectangles. Or cut apart netted bath poufs to make flat strips. Or cut the sides from woven fruit bags.

SAY: Today our Bible story is about a time when Jesus and his friends had breakfast together on the beach. But before they had breakfast, Jesus' friends went fishing and caught fish to eat. In Bible times, fishermen did not catch fish with fishing poles. They caught them with nets. Some people use nets to fish today.

- Tape a piece of netting in front of each child. Then lightly tape a piece of construction paper over the netting.

- Show the children how to rub over the paper with the sides of crayons (with papers removed). The pattern of the rubbing will show through onto the paper.

- Give each child a paper fish. Let the children glue the paper fish onto the construction paper.

SAY: Jesus' friends caught 153 fish. That's a lot of fish!

Fish in the Sea

Supplies: none

- Make sure the area from one side of the room to the other is free from obstacles.

- Have the children stand on one side of the room.

SAY: Today our Bible story is about a time when Jesus and his friends had breakfast together on the beach. But before they had breakfast, Jesus' friends went fishing and caught fish to eat. Pretend that I am a fisherman, and you are fish in the sea. You're going to swim from one side of the room to the other. But watch out! I'm going to try to catch you.

- Say the following poem. At the end of the poem, have the children pretend to swim from one side of the room to the other. Try to tag the children as they move. Any child who is tagged becomes a fisherman.

Fish in the ocean.	Swim as fast as you can
Fish in the sea.	or get caught by me.

Live the Bible

Heart Stamps

Supplies: cardboard paper towel rolls, scissors, washable paint, paper plates, construction paper, smocks, paper or plastic table covering

- Cut paper towel rolls into thirds. Flatten each roll so the roll makes a heart shape.

- Cover the table with paper or plastic, and have the children wear paint smocks.

- Pour washable paint onto paper plates.
- Give each child a piece of construction paper. Show the children how to hold the rolls, dip them into the paint, and then press the painted ends onto the paper.

ASK: What shape have we made? *(hearts)* What do hearts remind us of? *(love)*

SAY: After breakfast, Jesus asked Peter, "Peter, do you love me?" three times. Each time, Peter said, "Yes, I love you." Then Jesus told Peter to take care of Jesus' sheep. Jesus was calling people by a special nickname. Jesus called them sheep.

SAY: Jesus wanted Peter to love and take care of people, just like a shepherd takes care of the sheep. We can show our love for Jesus by taking care of others.

Play Dough Hearts

Supplies: play dough, heart cookie cutters

- Give each child some play dough.
- Show the children how to roll play dough into "snakes." Then show the children how to shape the "snakes" into hearts.

SAY: In our Bible story today, Jesus told Peter to love and care for others. Then Jesus called people by a special name. Jesus called them sheep. Jesus wanted Peter to take care of people, just like a shepherd takes care of the sheep.

- Let the children continue enjoy making hearts by making "snakes" and by using the heart cookie cutters.

ASK: What are some things we can do to show love and care to others?

Express Praise

Praise and Pray

Supplies: CD-ROM, CD player

- Sing with the children the song, "Hear Us As We Pray," from the CD-ROM.
- Encourage the children to name any prayer requests.

PRAY: Thank you, God, for Jesus. Help us show love to Jesus by taking care of others. Amen.

Blessing

Supplies: lip balm or olive oil

- Have the children stand in a circle.
- Go to each child and use the lip balm to draw a cross on the back of the child's hand. You can also dip your finger in a small amount of olive oil and use the oil to draw a cross.

SAY: Jesus is not on the cross or in the tomb. Jesus is alive. Jesus loves *(child's name)*.

- Continue until you have blessed each child.

Breakfast on the Beach

**Now hurry, go and tell his disciples, "He's been raised from the dead."
(Matthew 28:7)**

The Great Commission

Bible Verse: Now hurry, go and tell his disciples, "He's been raised from the dead." (Matthew 28:7)

Bible Story: Matthew 28:16-20

Bible Background

Today's story is the only post-resurrection appearance of Jesus included in the Gospel of Matthew. Matthew's story of Jesus appearing to the disciples isn't focused at all on proving to the disciples that Jesus has risen. Matthew assumes the disciples have already accepted this has occurred. Matthew has Jesus giving his disciples the authority to baptize, teach, and make disciples.

This story is commonly referred to as "The Great Commission." A commission can be a command to act in a certain way or the authority to act on behalf of another person. Here, both of these meanings are appropriate. Jesus knows he will no longer be with them, so he grants the disciples the authority to continue his work. This task is not a "Well, if you want to go ahead and do this" situation, however. Jesus is commanding the disciples. This is their job, to "go and make disciples of all nations." Although Jesus' ministry has been localized in a relatively small geographic area, his commission to the disciples is to spread the Word.

Devotion

As followers of Jesus, the Great Commission is for us, as well as the disciples. We are charged with spreading the Word. We are to tell people about Jesus' love. Jesus does not issue the Great Commission to the disciples and to us and then leave us on our own. Jesus left the disciples with a promise that extends to all of his followers, including us: "I myself will be with you every day."

As you once again prepare this week to follow the call God has placed on your life and share the good news about Jesus with the children in your care, remember Jesus' promise. You are never alone. When the unexpected question arises, when the supplies fall short, when the activity that worked so well at home falls apart in class, hang in there and remember that Jesus is always right there with you.

BASIC

Plan

Bible Beginnings
Welcome
Picture the Bible Story
Bible Puzzle
Bible Play

Into the Bible
Time for the Bible Story
Open the Bible
Experience the Bible Story
Say the Bible Verse

Bible Connections
Coffee Filter World
Bible Verse on the Move

Live the Bible
Megaphone Mania
Jesus Is Always with . . .

Express Praise
Praise and Pray
Blessing

Bible Beginnings

Welcome

Supplies: Class Pack—p. 8, CD-ROM, CD player, tape, offering basket

- Display the Bible Verse Picture (Class Pack—p. 8) at eye level.
- Play, "The B-I-B-L-E" (CD-ROM), as you welcome each child.
- Show the children where to place their offerings on the worship table.

SAY: Today our Bible story is about a time when Jesus told his friends to go to a mountain in a place called Galilee. Jesus promised his friends he would meet them on the mountain and tell them something important. Jesus told his friends to go all over the world to tell people that Jesus is alive and always with them.

- Point out the Bible Verse Picture, and say the Bible verse for the child.

Picture the Bible Story

Supplies: Leader Guide—p. 60, crayons or markers

- Photocopy "Go to All the World" for each child.
- Give each child a copy of the picture.

SAY: In today's Bible story, Jesus told his friends something important. Jesus told his friends to go all over the world to tell people that Jesus is alive and always with them.

- Encourage each child to decorate the picture with crayons or markers.

Bible Puzzle

Supplies: Bible Story Leaflet—Session 9, p. 4; crayons or markers

- Give each child a copy of "Go and Tell."
- Encourage the children to follow the directions to complete the activity.

SAY: In today's Bible story, Jesus told his friends something important. Jesus told his friends to go all over the world to tell people that Jesus is alive and always with them.

Bible Play

Supplies: blue and green play dough

SAY: Our Bible story is about a time when Jesus told his friends to go all over the world to tell people that Jesus is alive and always with them.

- Give each child a small portion of blue play dough and a small portion of green play dough.
- Let the children mix the two colors of play dough together.
- Show the children how to roll the mixed play dough into a ball to make a play-dough Earth.

Into the Bible

Time for the Bible Story

- Have the children follow you to your story area. Sing the following song as you lead the children. The song is sung to the tune of "Twinkle, Twinkle, Little Star."

SING: Go to people everywhere;
 tell them of my love and care.
 Listen to the words I say;
 I am with you every day.
 Go to people everywhere;
 tell them of my love and care.

- Have the children sit down.

SAY: Jesus told his friends to go all over the world to tell people that Jesus is alive and always with them.

Open the Bible

Supplies: Bible Basics Storybook—pp. 170–171

- Tell the children the story, "The Great Commission."

Experience the Bible Story

Supplies: CEB Bible; Bible Story Leaflet—Session 9, pp. 2-3

- Show the children the Bible.

TODAY'S BIBLE TOOL: Stories about Jesus are in the New Testament.

SAY: Our Bible is divided into two parts, the Old Testament and the New Testament. Stories about Jesus are in the New Testament.

- Show the children the beginning of the New Testament. Then show the children the Book of Matthew. Turn to the twenty-eighth chapter.

SAY: Our Bible story is about what happened when Jesus told his friends something important. It's chapter twenty-eight in the Book of Matthew. It is the very last chapter in the book.

- Place the Leaflet in your Bible. Tell the children the story, "The Great Commission" from the Bible Story Leaflet, and encourage them to do the motions as suggested.

ASK: How do you think Jesus' friends felt when they saw Jesus on the mountain? How do you think Jesus felt when he told them to go all over the world?

Say the Bible Verse

Supplies: Class Pack—p. 8, Leader Guide—p. 94

- Show the children the Bible Verse Picture. Repeat the verse for the children.
- Teach the children signs from American Sign Language (Leader Guide) to go along with the verse.
- Encourage the children to make the signs as they say the verse again.

Bible Connections

Coffee Filter World

Supplies: white coffee filters; blue and green washable markers; paintbrushes; cups or containers of water; paper or plastic table covering; optional: construction paper or paper plates, glue

- Cover the table with paper or plastic.

SAY: In today's Bible story, Jesus told his friends something important. Jesus told his friends to go all over the world to tell people that Jesus is alive and always with them. Let's make a world to help us remember what Jesus said.

- Give each child a coffee filter. Have each child spread the coffee filter out flat.
- Let each child color the coffee filter with blue and green markers. Encourage each child to completely cover the filter.
- Place cups or containers of water on the table for the children to share.
- Give each child a paintbrush. Show the children how to brush water all over the filter. The colors will run, making it look like the Earth as it is seen from outer space.
- Set the world filters aside to dry. You may want to let the children glue their dry filter worlds onto construction paper or onto the center of inexpensive paper plates.

Bible Verse on the Move

Supplies: none

- Have the children move to one side of the room. Make sure the area across to the opposite side of the room is free from any barriers.

SAY: Today our Bible story is about a time when Jesus told his friends to go all over the world and tell people Jesus is alive and always with them. Our Bible verse is what Jesus told the women who went to the empty tomb to tell his friends. Let's say the Bible verse together: "Now hurry, go and tell his disciples, 'He's been raised from the dead'" (Matthew 28:7). Listen as I call your name and say the Bible verse to you. Then move across the room like I've told you to move.

- Call each child by name and say the Bible verse. Substitute another movement word instead of the word "hurry." For instance, "Lucas, now hop, go and tell his disciples, 'He's been raised from the dead.'" Encourage Lucas to hop across the room.
- Continue with each child. Some suggested movement words are: march, tiptoe, take giant steps, gallop, walk backwards, crawl, jump, and so forth.
- End the game by having the children say the correct Bible verse with you and then hurrying back to the beginning side of the room.

Live the Bible

Megaphone Mania

Supplies: construction paper, colorful tape, crayons or markers, stickers

- Give each child a piece of construction paper and crayons to make a megaphone. Invite the children to decorate their papers with crayons, markers, and stickers.
- Show each child how to roll the paper into a cone by rolling one cone corner diagonally to the opposite corner. Adjust the ends of the cone. To make one side smaller, tighten the paper. To make one side larger, loosen the paper.
- Help each child tape the megaphone together along the seam.

SAY: Jesus told his friends to go all over the world and tell people that Jesus is alive and always with us. We are Jesus' friends. We can share the stories of Jesus with everyone. We can share God's love with everyone.

- Encourage the children to use their megaphones to share stories about Jesus. Give each child an opportunity to share her or his favorite Jesus story.
- If a child does not want to share a Jesus story, have the child hold up the megaphone and say, "Jesus is alive!"

Jesus Is Always with . . .

Supplies: plain paper, crayons or markers, googly eyes, glue

- At the top of a plain piece of paper, write, "Jesus is always with." Photocopy the page so that you have enough for each child.
- Give each child the page. Have each child place a hand (with fingers together) underneath the words. Trace the child's hand.
- Encourage the child to decorate the handprint to be her or his face. The palm can become the face and the fingers the hair.
- Give each child two googly eyes. Let the children glue the eyes onto their faces.
- As the children are working, go to each child and write the child's name underneath the handprint. Now the page reads, "Jesus is always with (name of child)."

Express Praise

Praise and Pray

Supplies: CD-ROM, CD player

- Sing with the children the song, "Hear Us As We Pray," from the CD-ROM. Encourage the children to name any prayer requests.

PRAY: Thank you, God, for Jesus. Thank you, that you and Jesus are always with us. Amen.

Blessing

Supplies: lip balm or olive oil

- Have the children stand in a circle. Go to each child and use the lip balm to draw a cross on the back of the child's hand. You can also dip your finger in a small amount of olive oil and use the oil to draw the cross.

SAY: Jesus is not on the cross or in the tomb. Jesus is alive. Jesus loves *(child's name)*.

- Continue until you have blessed each child.

Go to All the World

**Now hurry, go and tell his disciples, "He's been raised from the dead."
(Matthew 28:7)**

Believers Share

Bible Verse: They were all filled with the Holy Spirit. (Acts 2:4)

Bible Story: Acts 4:32-37

Bible Background

The early Christian believers were "one in heart and mind" (Acts 4:32). The believers considered their individual possessions and property as belonging to all of them—the entire community of believers. Everything was available for the common good.

A common fund was established under the guardianship of the apostles. Because of this general fund, everyone was taken care of and provided for, and no one was in need.

Barnabas was an important man in the community. Barnabas helped add to the common fund by selling a piece of land and donating the money from the sale. We begin to hear about Barnabas after this event. We learn that the name *Barnabas* means "one who encourages." Barnabas saw the good in people. Because of his encouraging spirit, many people came to believe in Jesus.

The sharing of the community resources shows that the first Christians had remarkable character. The first Christians were bound together by Christian love and fellowship. It appears they not only shared everything they had in common, but they actually wanted to share with each other.

Because the early Christians "were one in heart and mind," this very belief and action made an impression on the people who lived around them. Both the believers' ability to share and their love for each other did much to promote Christianity and make people want to become Christians.

Devotion

Barnabas was known for how he encouraged others. What are you saying and doing to encourage the children in your care? Many studies point out the importance of positive reenforcement for children as they develop self-esteem. You have a wonderful opportunity to add to their development. But what about you? What encouragement do you need? Look in a mirror. Imagine Jesus saying those exact encouraging words to you.

BASIC

Plan

Bible Beginnings
- Welcome
- Picture the Bible Story
- Bible Puzzle
- Bible Play

Into the Bible
- Time for the Bible Story
- Open the Bible
- Experience the Bible Story
- Say the Bible Verse

Bible Connections
- Money to Share
- Coat Relay

Live the Bible
- Sharing Art
- Sharing Food

Express Praise
- Praise and Pray
- Blessing

Bible Beginnings

Welcome

Supplies: Class Pack—p. 9, CD-ROM, CD player, tape, offering basket

• Display the Bible Verse Picture (Class Pack—p. 9) at eye level.

• Play, "The B-I-B-L-E" (CD-ROM), as you welcome each child.

• Show the children where to place their offerings on the worship table.

SAY: Today our Bible story is about how the first people who followed Jesus shared what they had with one another.

• Point out the Bible Verse Picture, and say the Bible verse for the children.

Picture the Bible Story

Supplies: Leader Guide—p. 66, crayons or markers

• Photocopy "Believers Share" for each child.

• Give each child a copy of the picture.

SAY: Today our Bible story is about how the first people who followed Jesus shared what they had with one another. One follower named Barnabas sold some land. He gave the money from the sale of the land to help other followers of Jesus.

• Encourage the children to decorate the picture with crayons or markers. Compliment the children on how well they are sharing the crayons or markers.

Bible Puzzle

Supplies: Bible Story Leaflet—Session 10, p. 4; crayons or markers

• Give each child a copy of "We Can Share."

• Encourage the children to each draw a picture of something they can share with a friend or family member.

SAY: Today our Bible story is about how the first people who followed Jesus shared what they had with one another.

ASK: What are some things we share here in our room? What are some things you share with your family? What are some things you can share with your friends?

Bible Play

Supplies: sand table or sand, shallow tray, plastic tub, or box lid; paper or plastic table covering

• If you do not have a sand table, pour clean sand into a shallow tray, plastic tub, or box lid. Place the sand on a paper or plastic table covering.

• Show the children how to draw a simple fish outline in the sand.

SAY: Today our Bible story is about the first people who followed Jesus. Sometimes the followers used a secret picture to tell other followers where they were. They would draw a simple fish in the dirt or sand.

Into the Bible

Time for the Bible Story

- Have the children follow you to your story area. Sing the following song as you lead the children. The song is sung to the tune of "God Is So Good."

SING: They were all filled,
they were all filled,
they were all filled
with the Holy Spirit.

- Have the children sit down.

SAY: We just sang our Bible verse. Let's say it together: "They were all filled with the Holy Spirit" (Acts 2:4).

Open the Bible

Supplies: Bible Basics Storybook—pp. 266–267

- Tell the children the story, "Believers Share."

Experience the Bible Story

Supplies: CEB Bible; Bible Story Leaflet—Session 10, pp. 2–3

- Show the children the Bible.

TODAY'S BIBLE TOOL: Stories about people who followed Jesus are in the New Testament.

SAY: Our Bible is divided into two parts, the Old Testament and the New Testament. Stories about Jesus and people who followed Jesus are in the New Testament.

- Show the children the beginning of the New Testament. Then show the children the Book of Acts. Turn to the fourth chapter.

SAY: Our Bible story is about how the first people who followed Jesus shared what they had with one another. It's chapter four in the Book of Acts.

- Place the Leaflet in your Bible. Tell the children the story, "Believers Share" from the Bible Story Leaflet, and encourage them to do the motions as suggested.

ASK: How do you think Barnabas felt when he gave the money from his land to help others? How does it feel to share with your friends?

Say the Bible Verse

Supplies: Class Pack—p. 9, Leader Guide—p. 95

- Show the children the Bible Verse Picture. Repeat the verse for the children.
- Teach the children signs from American Sign Language (Leader Guide) to go along with the verse.
- Encourage the children to make the signs as they say the verse again.

Bible Connections

Money to Share

Supplies: play or real quarters, dimes, nickels, and pennies; paper; tape; crayons with papers removed

SAY: In our Bible story today, a follower of Jesus named Barnabas sold some land and then gave the money to help other followers of Jesus.

ASK: What do you think the other followers bought with the money? *(food, clothing, medicine, and so forth)*

- Mix up the coins and place them in one pile. Let the children sort the coins.
- Let each child choose two or more coins. Use a roll of tape to tape the coins to the table in front of each child. Lightly tape a piece of paper over the coins.
- Show the children how to use the sides of the crayons (with papers removed) to rub over the paper. The coins will show on the paper with the crayon rubbings.

Coat Relay

Supplies: an adult-size coat or sweater for each relay line

- Have the children line up on one side of the room in relay lines.
- Place a chair on one side of the room for each relay line. Place a coat on each chair.

SAY: Our Bible story today is about how the first followers of Jesus shared what they had. They shared things like food and money and clothes. Let's play a game where we share coats.

- Explain to the children that the first person in line will hop across the room to the chair, put on the coat, and then sit in the chair. Next, the child will stand up, take off the coat, place the coat back on the chair, and then race to the next child in line.
- If you have a small group of children, you can have one relay line. Vary how each child moves to the coat (march, tiptoe, walk backwards, jump, take giant steps).

Live the Bible

Sharing Art

Supplies: CD-ROM, CD player, mural paper, crayons or markers, table

- Cover the top of a table with mural paper.

SAY: Today our Bible story is about how the first followers of Jesus shared what they had with one another. We share what we have in this room with one another. Let's share paper and crayons together to make a large picture.

- Let each child choose one crayon or marker.
- Have the children hold their crayons or markers and stand around the table.
- Play, "The B-I-B-L-E" (CD-ROM). Have the children march around the table as the music plays.

- Stop the music and have the children stop marching. Encourage the children to use their crayons or markers to draw on the paper in front of them.
- After a few minutes, start the music again and have the children march around the table.
- Stop the music when the children are in different places at the table. Have the children draw on the paper at their new spots.
- Continue the game until you have a beautiful piece of sharing art.

Sharing Food

Supplies: things to go in a trail mix, such as different kinds of cereal, raisins, chocolate chips, banana chips, pretzels, and fish crackers; bowls; spoons or scoops; resealable plastic bags; hand-washing supplies

- Have the children wash their hands.
- Place the different items in bowls with spoons or scoops.

SAY: In our Bible story today, the first followers of Jesus shared what they had with one another. One of the things they shared was food. Let's make trail-mix bags. You can make one bag for yourself and one that you can share with a friend or someone in your family.

- Give each child two resealable plastic bags. Show the children how to use the spoon or scoop to place the items in the bags.
- Let the children choose which items they would like to have in their trail mixes.
- Securely seal the plastic bags. Let the children shake the bags to mix the ingredients.

TIP: Check for allergies before handling or serving food with children.

Express Praise

Praise and Pray

Supplies: CD-ROM, CD player

- Sing with the children the song, "Hear Us As We Pray," from the CD-ROM.
- Encourage the children to name any prayer requests.

PRAY: Thank you, God, for stories about followers of Jesus. Help us show our love for Jesus by sharing with others. Amen.

Blessing

Supplies: Leader Guide—p. 95

- Teach the children the American Sign Language sign for *spirit* (p. 95). Go to each child and sign the word *spirit*.

SAY: *(Child's name),* may God's Spirit be with you.

- Continue until you have blessed each child.

TIP: If you get questions about the meaning of God's Spirit, you might say God's Spirit is the feeling you have when you know God is with you and that God loves you.

Believers Share

They were all filled with the Holy Spirit. (Acts 2:4)

Choosing the Seven

Bible Verse: They were all filled with the Holy Spirit. (Acts 2:4)

Bible Story: Acts 6:1-7

Bible Background

The Bible story for today's lesson is one that may not be familiar to you. In the sixth chapter of Acts, we read the story of the early church choosing seven men to oversee the daily distribution of food to the poor. The story is a short one, and the premise seems simple and straightforward. However, there is much to be learned from these seven verses.

The story begins by describing a conflict between the two groups in the early church. How the particular conflict developed is unstated, but we're told that the issue involves the case of some widows not receiving enough food during the daily distribution of food. Right from the start, the story contains interesting information about the early church.

First of all, disagreement sometimes occurred between groups in church. This may serve as reassurance to those who have seen a similar occurrence in their own church. Because the church is comprised of humans, none of us is perfect; differences of opinion will occur. When conflicts occur in the church today, we can follow the example of the early church and work together to find a solution.

Secondly, there was a system in the early church that provided for food distribution so that everyone had enough to eat and no one went hungry. Right from the beginning, Christians have followed Jesus' example of helping others. Helping and serving others have always been important aspects of life as a Christian.

Devotion

The early church leaders came up with a solution to the conflict that had arisen. They decided to have the congregation choose certain members to oversee the food distribution. Here is recognition that while we're all called to do God's work, none of us can do everything. There are plenty of ministry opportunities to go around, even for young children. Encourage the children in your group to help at church. They can help pick up toys, make cards for persons who are sick or lonely, and greet people in worship. As a teacher, you are an example for your children. Thank you for serving God by teaching.

BASIC

Plan

Bible Beginnings
Welcome
Picture the Bible Story
Bible Puzzle
Bible Play

Into the Bible
Time for the Bible Story
Open the Bible
Experience the Bible Story
Say the Bible Verse

Bible Connections
Seven
Serve the Widows

Live the Bible
Who Helps at Church?
Add a Name

Express Praise
Praise and Pray
Blessing

Bible Beginnings

Welcome

Supplies: Class Pack—p. 9, CD-ROM, CD player, tape, offering basket

• Display the Bible Verse Picture (Class Pack—p. 9) at eye level.

• Play, "The B-I-B-L-E" (CD-ROM), as you welcome each child.

• Show the children where to place their offerings on the worship table.

SAY: Today our Bible story is about seven men who were chosen to be helpers to the followers of Jesus. The seven helped by doing kind things for others.

• Point out the Bible Verse Picture, and say the Bible verse for the child.

Picture the Bible Story

Supplies: Leader Guide—p. 72, crayons or markers

• Photocopy "Choosing the Seven" for each child.

• Give each child a copy of the picture.

SAY: Today our Bible story is about seven men who were chosen to be helpers to the followers of Jesus. The seven helped by doing kind things for others.

• Encourage the children to decorate the picture with crayons or markers.

Bible Puzzle

Supplies: Bible Story Leaflet—Session 11, p. 4; crayons, markers, stickers, or non-permanent ink pads and hand wipes

• Give each child a copy of "Seven."

• Encourage the children to add seven stickers, make seven thumbprints, or draw seven hearts in the number

SAY: Seven is an important number in today's Bible story. Today our Bible story is about seven men who were chosen to be helpers to the followers of Jesus.

Bible Play

Supplies: sand table or sand, shallow tray, plastic tub, or box lid; paper or plastic table covering

• If you do not have a sand table, pour clean sand into a shallow tray, plastic tub, or box lid. Place the sand on a paper or plastic table covering.

• Show the children how to draw a simple fish outline in the sand.

SAY: Today our Bible story is about the first people who followed Jesus. Sometimes the followers used a secret picture to tell other followers where they were. They would draw a simple fish in the dirt or sand.

Into the Bible

Time for the Bible Story

- Have the children follow you to your story area. Sing the following song as you lead the children. The song is sung to the tune of "God Is So Good."

SING: They were all filled,
 they were all filled,
 they were all filled
 with the Holy Spirit.

- Have the children sit down.

SAY: We just sang our Bible verse. Let's say it together: "They were all filled with the Holy Spirit" (Acts 2:4).

Open the Bible

Supplies: Bible Basics Storybook—pp. 268–269

- Tell the children the story, "Choosing the Seven."

Experience the Bible Story

Supplies: CEB Bible; Bible Story Leaflet—Session 11, pp. 2–3

- Show the children the Bible.

TODAY'S BIBLE TOOL: Stories about people who followed Jesus are in the New Testament.

SAY: Our Bible is divided into two parts, the Old Testament and the New Testament. Stories about Jesus and people who followed Jesus are in the New Testament.

- Show the children the beginning of the New Testament. Then show the children the Book of Acts. Turn to the sixth chapter.

SAY: Our Bible story is about how seven men who were chosen to be helpers to the followers of Jesus. It's chapter six in the Book of Acts.

- Place the Leaflet in your Bible. Tell the children the story, "Believers Share" from the Bible Story Leaflet, and encourage them to count with you.

ASK: How do you think it felt to be one of the chosen men?

Say the Bible Verse

Supplies: Class Pack—p. 9, Leader Guide—p. 95

- Show the children the Bible Verse Picture. Repeat the verse for the children.
- Teach the children signs from American Sign Language (Leader Guide) to go along with the verse.
- Encourage the children to make the signs as they say the verse again.

Bible Connections

Seven

Supplies: posterboard, masking tape or painters' tape, washable paint, sponges, shallow trays, plastic or paper table covering, smocks, table, hand-washing supplies

- Cover the table with paper or plastic. Pour washable paint into shallow trays.
- Have the children wear paint smocks to protect their clothing.
- Place the posterboard on the table. Use masking tape or painters' tape to stick a large number "7" on the posterboard.
- Move the paint trays so they are within easy reach.

SAY: Today our Bible story is about seven men who were chosen to be helpers to the followers of Jesus. The seven helped by doing kind things for others.

- Show the children how to dip the sponges into the paint trays and then press the sponges onto the posterboard. Encourage the children to completely cover over the posterboard (including the tape) with the paint.
- Have the children gather around the "7" painting. Carefully remove the tape. The number "7" will be visible on the painting.
- Have the children wash their hands.

Serve the Widows

Supplies: tray, towel or piece of cloth, plastic food items or unbreakable food packages

- Place the food items on a tray.
- Have the children sit in a circle.

SAY: In today's Bible story, seven men were chosen to help serve food to all the widows. Let's pretend we are the widows. Look at the food we're serving today.

- Show the tray to the children. Have the children name each of the food items.
- Cover the tray with a cloth or towel and have the children cover their eyes.
- Slip one of the food items and hide it in the room where it can easily be found.
- Have the children uncover their eyes.

ASK: What's missing?

- Help the children remember and identify the missing item.

Live the Bible

Who Helps at Church?

Supplies: none

SAY: Today our Bible story is about seven men who were chosen to be helpers to the friends of Jesus. The seven helped by doing kind things for others. We have helpers here at our church. Let's play a game to guess our child helpers.

- Sing, "Do You Know?" to the tune of "The Muffin Man" and do the motions. Encourage the children to sing and do the motions with you.

SING: Do you know who teaches you, teaches you, teaches you? *(Tap the side of your head.)* Do you know who teaches you when you go to church? *(teacher)*

Do you know who sings for you, sings for you, sings for you? *(Cup your hands around your mouth.)* Do you know who sings for you when you go to church? *(choir member)*

Do you know who welcomes you, welcomes you, welcomes you? *(Shake one another's hands.)* Do you know who welcomes you when you go to church? *(usher)*

Do you know who rocks the babies, rocks the babies, rocks the babies? *(Pretend to rock a baby.)* Do you know who rocks the babies when you go to church? *(nursery worker)*

Add a Name

Supplies: none

(Your name) read an announcement in the (name of church) bulletin. "Helpers Needed!" said the announcement. (Your name) said she (he) would help by teaching the (name of your group). (Name one or two children) said they would help by putting the crayons and markers away. (Name one child) said he (she) would help (name one child) pick up the blocks. (Name three or four children) said their families would plant flowers in the (name of church) garden. (Name one or two children) said they would help their moms and dads hand out bulletins before worship. (Name three or four children) said they would sing in the children's choir. (Name two or three children) said they would make cards to send to people who were sick. (Name two or three children) said they would bring in cans of food for the food pantry. "Wow!" said (your name). It takes many people to help (name of church).

Express Praise

Praise and Pray

Supplies: CD-ROM, CD player

- Sing with the children the song, "Hear Us As We Pray," from the CD-ROM.
- Encourage the children to name any prayer requests.

PRAY: Thank you, God, for followers of Jesus. Thank you for church helpers. I want to be a helper too. Amen.

Blessing

Supplies: Leader Guide—p. 95

- Teach the children the American Sign Language sign for *spirit* (p. 95).
- Go to each child and sign the word *spirit*.

SAY: *(Child's name),* may God's Spirit be with you.

- Continue until you have blessed each child.

Choosing the Seven

They were all filled with the Holy Spirit. (Acts 2:4)

Philip and the Ethiopian

Bible Verse: They were all filled with the Holy Spirit. (Acts 2:4)

Bible Story: Acts 8:26-40

Bible Background

Today's Bible story is about the Spirit at work in the life of Philip, one of the seven men chosen to be a deacon. The story is the interaction between Philip and the Ethiopian is an example of the amazing things that happen when followers of Jesus allow the Spirit to guide their actions and their words.

The Ethiopian in the story was an important official who was responsible for the treasury of the Ethiopian queen. In spite of his status, Jews at that time would have considered him an outsider for two reasons. Most Israelites would have treated him as an outcast because of where he lived and because he was a eunuch. His castration excluded him for the religious assembly and because he lived far from Jerusalem, pilgrimage to the Holy City would have been difficult. In spite of this, the Ethiopian man was seeking God. He had been to Jerusalem to worship and was on his way home when the Spirit sent Philip his way.

Philip, a follower of Jesus, had been preaching in Samaria when the Spirit, in the form of an angel, told him to take the road leading from Jerusalem to Gaza. On that road, Philip encountered the chariot carrying the Ethiopian man. The Spirit guided Philip to keep up with the chariot. As Philip ran by the chariot, he heard the Ethiopian reading aloud as was customary at the time. Philip recognized that the man was reading from the scroll of Isaiah. Philip asked the man if he understood what he was reading, and the man invited him to explain it. At this invitation, Philip told the Ethiopian about Jesus. To one who was considered an outcast, hearing about Jesus who welcomed society's outcasts must have been amazing. The Ethiopian man ended up asking Philip to baptize him before the Spirit led Philip elsewhere.

Devotion

Reflect on your life and your call to teach. Are you open to the Holy Spirit being revealed in the questions and understanding of the children? Are you open to following the Holy Spirit wherever it leads you with the children? Pray for the Holy Spirit to be with you each Sunday. Become aware of the situations in which you see the Holy Spirit at work in the children or in yourself. Write those situations down and refer to them later as you evaluate your day's experience with the children.

BASIC

Plan

Bible Beginnings
- Welcome
- Picture the Bible Story
- Bible Puzzle
- Bible Play

Into the Bible
- Time for the Bible Story
- Open the Bible
- Experience the Bible Story
- Say the Bible Verse

Bible Connections
- Make a Scroll
- Drive Your Chariot

Live the Bible
- Thank You for Teaching Me!
- Catch and Tell

Express Praise
- Praise and Pray
- Blessing

Bible Beginnings

Welcome

Supplies: Class Pack—p. 9, CD-ROM, CD player, tape, offering basket

• Display the Bible Verse Picture (Class Pack—p. 9) at eye level.

• Play, "The B-I-B-L-E" (CD-ROM), as you welcome each child.

• Show the children where to place their offerings on the worship table.

SAY: Today our Bible story is about Philip, a follower of Jesus who was chosen to be one of the seven helpers. Philip meets a man riding in a chariot.

• Point out the Bible Verse Picture, and say the Bible verse for the child.

Picture the Bible Story

Supplies: Leader Guide—p. 78, crayons or markers

• Photocopy "Philip and the Ethiopian" for each child.

• Give each child a copy of the picture.

SAY: Today our Bible story is about Philip, a follower of Jesus who was chosen to be one of the seven helpers. Philip meets a man riding in a chariot.

ASK: How did you come to church today? Did any of you ride in a chariot?

SAY: We don't use chariots today, but people did travel in chariots in Bible times. When Philip met the man riding in the chariot, he told the man about Jesus.

• Encourage the children to decorate the picture with crayons or markers.

Bible Puzzle

Supplies: Bible Story Leaflet—Session 12, p. 4; crayons or markers

• Give each child a copy of "Help Philip Follow the Path."

• Encourage each child to use a finger or a crayon to complete the maze.

SAY: Today our Bible story is about Philip, a follower of Jesus who was chosen to be one of the seven helpers. Philip meets a man riding in a chariot. Philip told the man about Jesus.

Bible Play

Supplies: sand table or sand, shallow tray, plastic tub, or box lid; paper or plastic table covering

• If you do not have a sand table, pour clean sand into a shallow tray, plastic tub, or box lid. Place the sand on a paper or plastic table covering.

• Show the children how to draw a simple fish outline in the sand.

SAY: Today our Bible story is about the first people who followed Jesus. Sometimes the followers used a secret picture to tell other followers where they were. They would draw a simple fish in the dirt or sand.

Into the Bible

Time for the Bible Story

- Have the children follow you to your story area. Sing the following song as you lead the children. The song is sung to the tune of "God Is So Good."

SING: They were all filled,
 they were all filled,
 they were all filled
 with the Holy Spirit.

- Have the children sit down.

SAY: We just sang our Bible verse. Let's say it together: "They were all filled with the Holy Spirit" (Acts 2:4).

Open the Bible

Supplies: Bible Basics Storybook—pp. 270-271

- Tell the children the story, "Philip and the Ethiopian."

Experience the Bible Story

Supplies: CEB Bible; Bible Story Leaflet—Session 12, pp. 2-3; paper or card stock; marker

- Use a marker to write a large "P" on a piece of paper or card stock. Show the children the Bible.

TODAY'S BIBLE TOOL: Stories about people who followed Jesus are in the New Testament.

SAY: Our Bible is divided into two parts, the Old Testament and the New Testament. Stories about Jesus and people who followed Jesus are in the New Testament.

- Show the children the beginning of the New Testament. Then show the children the Book of Acts. Turn to the eighth chapter.

SAY: Our Bible story is about Philip and a man from Ethiopia. It's chapter eight in the Book of Acts.

- Hold up the letter "P."

SAY: The name Philip begins with the letter "P." When I hold up this sign, I want you to say the name Philip.

- Place the Leaflet in your Bible. Tell the children the story, "Philip and the Ethiopian" from the Bible Story Leaflet. Encourage them to say the name Philip each time you hold up the sign.

ASK: How do you think the man from Ethiopia felt when Philip told him about Jesus?

Say the Bible Verse

Supplies: Class Pack—p. 9, Leader Guide—p. 95

- Show the children the Bible Verse Picture. Repeat the verse for the children.
- Teach the children signs from American Sign Language (Leader Guide) to go along with the verse. Encourage the children to make the signs as they say the verse again.

Bible Connections

Make a Scroll

Supplies: plain paper, crayons or markers, ribbon or yarn, scissors

- Cut ribbon or yarn into twelve-inch lengths.

SAY: Today our Bible story is about Philip, a follower of Jesus. Philip meets a man riding in a chariot. The man is reading a scroll. Philip helps the man understand what he is reading. Let's make a scroll.

- Give each child a piece of plain paper. Encourage the children to draw a picture of today's Bible story. Older children may write today's Bible verse.
- Show each child how to crumple the paper into a ball and then smooth it out again. Have the children do this several times. This will make the paper soft and pliable.
- Help each child roll the two ends of the paper toward the center to make a scroll.
- Tie a ribbon or piece of yarn around the scroll to keep it closed.

Drive Your Chariot

Supplies: none

- Have the children move to an open area of the room.

SAY: Today our Bible story is about Philip, a follower of Jesus. Philip meets a man riding in a chariot. Philip helps the man understand what he is reading. Let's pretend we are driving chariots.

- Have the children gallop around the room.

SAY: Great! Now when I say, "Giddyup!" you may gallop around the room. But when I say, "Whoa!" everyone must stop and freeze. Then we will say our Bible verse together: "They were all filled with the Holy Spirit" (Acts 2:4).

- Say, "Giddyup!" and Whoa!" several times.

Live the Bible

Thank You for Teaching Me!

Supplies: construction paper, crayons or markers, stickers

- Help each child fold a piece of construction paper in half to make a card.

SAY: In today's story, Philip taught the man from Ethiopia about Jesus.

ASK: Who has taught you about Jesus?

SAY: Let's make cards to thank the people who teach us about Jesus.

- Encourage older children to write, "Thank you for teaching me!" inside their cards.

- Help younger children write the statement, or write the statement on plain paper and photocopy enough for the younger children. Let the children glue the copy inside their cards.
- Invite the children to decorate their cards using crayons or markers and stickers.
- Encourage the children to give their cards to people who have taught them about Jesus.
- Enjoy receiving lots of cards!

TIP: If you don't want to make individual cards, you can have the children make a thank-you mural to display in the hall.

Catch and Tell

Supplies: ball, beanbag, or pair of rolled-up socks

- Have the children stand in a circle.

SAY: Philip told the man from Ethiopia about Jesus.

ASK: What is something you can tell others about Jesus?

SAY: I'm going to toss this ball *(beanbag, sock roll)* to someone in the circle. When you catch the ball, tell everyone what you want us to know about Jesus.

- Toss the ball (beanbag, sock roll) to one of the children in the circle. Encourage that child to tell something about Jesus. You may need to ask questions like, "When do we celebrate Jesus' birthday?" or "Did Jesus like children?" to help them with their answers.
- Have the child toss the ball back to you.
- Continue until every child has an opportunity to catch the ball and give an answer.

Express Praise

Praise and Pray

Supplies: CD-ROM, CD player

- Sing with the children the song, "Hear Us As We Pray," from the CD-ROM.
- Encourage the children to name any prayer requests.

PRAY: Thank you, God, for people who teach us about Jesus. Help us teach others about Jesus. Amen.

Blessing

Supplies: Leader Guide—p. 95

- Teach the children the American Sign Language sign for *spirit* (p. 95).
- Go to each child and sign the word *spirit*.

SAY: *(Child's name),* may God's Spirit be with you.

- Continue until you have blessed each child.

Philip and the Ethiopian

They were all filled with the Holy Spirit. (Acts 2:4)

First Called "Christians"

Bible Verse: They were all filled with the Holy Spirit. (Acts 2:4)

Bible Story: Acts 11:19-30

Bible Background

The name *Christian* was first used in Antioch in a sarcastic and derogatory way; but as often happens, what was meant for bad for Christians turned into something good.

The city of Antioch in Syria was the third largest city in the Roman Empire and home to almost one million people. It was a melting pot of people from the East, the West, the Greeks and Romans, the Semitic people, and the Arabian people. All theses different races and cultures had come together in Antioch. Antioch was a city of paradox—it was known as a city with loose morals—and yet, it had a large and growing Christian community.

It was in Antioch that this faith community grew among the Gentiles. Eventually, Antioch became known as a Christian stronghold. Paul made Antioch his headquarters, and from Antioch he would travel out to all the known world.

At this time, Barnabas acted as a mentor to Paul. The two men stayed in Antioch, teaching and preaching about Jesus for about a year. When Agabus, Judean prophet, came from Jerusalem to Antioch and predicted a famine in Jerusalem, the followers of Jesus in Jerusalem turned to the followers in Antioch. Paul and Barnabas collected money and took it to Judea (where Jerusalem is located).

The fish symbol has been added to this lesson on early Christians. The fish symbol is one of the most recognizable symbols of the faith. It's found on cars, business cards, and more. The symbol is based on the Greek words for Jesus Christ, God's Son, Savior. When you put the first letter of the Greek words together, it's ICHTHUS, the Greek word for fish. It's thought that early Christians used the symbol as a secret sign. When Christians saw a fish painted on a door or drawn in the sand, they knew they were safe.

Devotion

What groups do you identify with? Do you claim Christian as one of your identities? Naming yourself Christian can become a filter through which you view the world. The good news about Jesus has been handed down from generation to generation for nearly two thousand years. The news of God's love has traveled from Jesus' disciples to the early church all the way to us. Now it's time for us to pass on the good news!

BASIC

Plan

Bible Beginnings
- Welcome
- Picture the Bible Story
- Bible Puzzle
- Bible Play

Into the Bible
- Time for the Bible Story
- Open the Bible
- Experience the Bible Story
- Say the Bible Verse

Bible Connections
- Sign of the Fish
- Find the Fish

Live the Bible
- Beaded Fish
- I'm a Christian

Express Praise
- Praise and Pray
- Blessing

Bible Beginnings

Welcome

Supplies: Class Pack—p. 9, CD-ROM, CD player, tape, offering basket

- Display the Bible Verse Picture (Class Pack—p. 9) at eye level.
- Play, "The B-I-B-L-E" (CD-ROM), as you welcome each child.
- Show the children where to place their offerings on the worship table.

SAY: In our Bible story today, the followers of Jesus are first called Christians.

- Point out the Bible Verse Picture, and say the Bible verse for the child.

Picture the Bible Story

Supplies: Leader Guide—p. 84, crayons or markers

- Photocopy "The First Christians" for each child. Make two extra photocopies—one for the "Find the Fish" game (p. 82), and one for the "I'm a Christian" activity (p. 83).
- Give each child a copy of the picture.

SAY: In our Bible story today, the followers of Jesus are first called Christians. It was dangerous to be a Christian, and sometimes they had to hide to stay safe. The Christians used a secret picture to tell other Christians who they were. They would draw a simple fish in the dirt or sand.

- Invite the children to decorate the inside of the fish picture with crayons or markers.

TIP: Save the decorated pictures to use after the Bible story.

Bible Puzzle

Supplies: Bible Story Leaflet—Session 13, p. 4; crayons or markers

- Give each child a copy of "Find the Hidden Fish." Encourage the children to find five fish hidden in the picture.

SAY: In our Bible story today, the followers of Jesus are first called Christians. It was dangerous to be a Christian, and sometimes they had to hide to stay safe. The Christians used a secret picture to tell other Christians who they were. They would draw a simple fish in the dirt or sand.

Bible Play

Supplies: sand table or sand, shallow tray, plastic tub, or box lid; paper or plastic table covering

- If you do not have a sand table, pour clean sand into a shallow tray, plastic tub, or box lid. Place the sand on a paper or plastic table covering.
- Show the children how to draw a simple fish outline in the sand.

SAY: In our Bible story today, the followers of Jesus are first called Christians. It was dangerous to be a Christian, and sometimes they had to hide to stay safe. The Christians used a secret picture to tell other Christians who they were. They would draw a simple fish in the dirt or sand.

Into the Bible

Time for the Bible Story

- Have the children follow you to your story area. Sing the following song as you lead the children. The song is sung to the tune of "God Is So Good."

SING: They were all filled,
they were all filled,
they were all filled
with the Holy Spirit.

- Have the children sit down.

SAY: We just sang our Bible verse. Let's say it together: "They were all filled with the Holy Spirit" (Acts 2:4).

Open the Bible

Supplies: Bible Basics Storybook—pp. 280-281

- Tell the children the story, "First Called 'Christians.'"

Experience the Bible Story

Supplies: CEB Bible; Bible Story Leaflet—Session 13, pp. 2-3

- Show the children the Bible.

TODAY'S BIBLE TOOL: Stories about people who followed Jesus are in the New Testament.

SAY: Our Bible is divided into two parts, the Old Testament and the New Testament. Stories about Jesus and people who followed Jesus are in the New Testament.

- Show the children the beginning of the New Testament. Then show the children the Book of Acts. Turn to the eleventh chapter.

SAY: Our Bible story is about the followers of Jesus who lived in a city called Antioch. These followers were the very first people to be called Christian. The story is chapter eleven in the Book of Acts.

- Place the Leaflet in your Bible. Tell the children the story, "First Called 'Christians'" from the Bible Story Leaflet. Encourage them to do the motions as suggested.

ASK: How do you think the followers of Jesus felt when people started calling them by the name Christian?

Say the Bible Verse

Supplies: Class Pack—p. 9, Leader Guide—p. 95

- Show the children the Bible Verse Picture. Repeat the verse for the children.
- Teach the children signs from American Sign Language (Leader Guide) to go along with the verse. Encourage the children to make the signs as they say the verse again.

Bible Connections

Sign of the Fish

Supplies: fish pictures made earlier, glue, glue brushes or cotton swabs, shallow containers, fine sand or colored sand, box lid or baking tray

- Pour glue into shallow containers.

SAY: The followers of Jesus used the fish as a secret sign. The fish let them know it was safe to talk about Jesus.

- Give the children their fish pictures they decorated earlier.
- Show the children how to dip a glue brush or a cotton swab into the glue and then spread the glue along the outline of the fish.
- Let the children take turns placing their fish pictures in a box lid or baking tray. Help the children sprinkle fine sand or colored sand over the glue. Shake off the excess sand into a trash can.
- Set the pictures flat to dry.

Find the Fish

Supplies: Leader Guide—p. 84

- Photocopy one copy of "The First Christians" (p. 84), if not done previously.
- Have the children cover their eyes with their hands. Hide the fish picture somewhere in the room (or in another safe place).
- Have the children open their eyes.

WHISPER: Shh! Everyone, be quiet. We don't want anyone to see or hear us. We want to meet with the Christians in Antioch, but our meeting is secret. We have to find the secret fish sign. Everyone, tiptoe around the room and look for the fish.

- Have the children move around the room until they find the sign.
- If you have an older group of children, change this to a game of hot or cold. Send one child out of the room with another teacher, or have one child cover her or his eyes. Hide the fish picture somewhere in the room. Have the child open his or her eyes and look for the picture. When the child moves closer to the picture, have the other children shout, "Hot!" When the child moves farther away from the picture, have the other children shout, "Cold!"

Live the Bible

Beaded Fish

Supplies: beads, chenille stems

SAY: Today our Bible story is about when the followers of Jesus were first called Christians. The fish symbol helps us remember those first Christians. The fish symbol also tells people today that we are Christians.

- Give each child a chenille stem.
- Show the children how to bend a chenille stem into a U shape.
- Let the children thread beads onto their chenille stems, leaving approximately one to two inches on each end without beads.
- Twist the empty ends of the chenille stem together. This will make the fish's tail.

I'm a Christian

Supplies: Leader Guide—p. 84, nonpermanent stamp pads, magnifying glasses, hand wipes

- Photocopy one copy of "The First Christians" (p. 84), if not done previously.

SAY: Today our Bible story is about when the followers of Jesus were first called Christians. The fish symbol helps us remember those first Christians.

- Let the children work together to fill in the fish symbol with their thumbprints.
- Show the children how to press a thumb onto the ink pad and then inside the fish.
- Have the children clean their thumbs with hand wipes to remove the ink.
- Encourage the children to look at their thumbprints with a magnifying glass.

SAY: Each one of us has different thumbprints because each one of us is special. But even though we are all different in some way, we're also alike in some way.

ASK: How are we different? How are we alike? What about followers of Jesus—how are they different? How are they alike?

SAY: Followers of Jesus are all called Christians, just like those first followers of Jesus.

Express Praise

Praise and Pray

Supplies: CD-ROM, CD player

- Sing with the children the song, "Hear Us As We Pray," from the CD-ROM.
- Encourage the children to name any prayer requests.

PRAY: Thank you, God, for the first people who were called Christians. I'm happy to be a Christian too. Amen.

Blessing

Supplies: Leader Guide—p. 95

- Teach the children the American Sign Language sign for *spirit* (p. 95).
- Go to each child and sign the word *spirit*.

SAY: *(Child's name),* may God's Spirit be with you.

- Continue until you have blessed each child.

The First Christians

They were all filled with the Holy Spirit. (Acts 2:4)

Pentecost

Bible Verse: They were all filled with the Holy Spirit. (Acts 2:4)

Bible Story: Acts 2:1-41

Bible Background

Although as Christians we celebrate Pentecost as the "birthday of the church," the day God sent the Spirit to the followers of Jesus, Pentecost is not a holiday that originated with Christianity. Pentecost was a Jewish festival more commonly known as the Feast of Weeks. Pentecost was one of three pilgrimage feasts when Jews gathered in Jerusalem. It was to celebrate Pentecost that the disciples and other followers of Jesus were gathered together in Jerusalem.

While they were gathered in Jerusalem, the Spirit arrived. The arrival of the Spirit was not a calm quiet event, but appeared sounding like a violent wind and looking like tongues of fire. The believers could speak in different languages. The crowd outside the house was first confused by these happenings, but then they were astonished! Peter and others spoke about the great working of God in the people's own native languages. This was indeed a strange occurrence since the disciples were often teased and mocked because of their Galilean accents.

The Spirit's arrival in Jerusalem on the Day of Pentecost is a fulfillment of prophecy and an answer to the community's expectant prayers. Jesus promised to send the disciples an advocate, a helper, and now it had arrived.

The Spirit did not come just to the disciples, but to each person gathered there. It appears there is plenty of Spirit to go around. It is this Spirit that empowered God's people to continue to spread the good news of Jesus all over the world. The experience of this first Pentecost shows that Jesus Christ is for all people all over the world.

Devotion

The Spirit is still active and at work in the world. We may not hear rushing wind or see tongues of fire, but God's Spirit continues to empower us to do God's work. Invite the Holy Spirit to work within you as you teach, prepare, and love children into the faith.

BASIC

Plan

Bible Beginnings
Welcome
Picture the Bible Story
Bible Puzzle
Bible Play

Into the Bible
Time for the Bible Story
Open the Bible
Experience the Bible Story
Say the Bible Verse

Bible Connections
Pentecost Hats
Pentecost Tag

Live the Bible
Pentecost Party
Pentecost Praise

Express Praise
Praise and Pray
Blessing

Bible Beginnings

Welcome

Supplies: Class Pack—p. 9, CD-ROM, CD player, tape, offering basket

• Display the Bible Verse Picture (Class Pack—p. 9) at eye level.

• Play, "The B-I-B-L-E" (CD-ROM), as you welcome each child.

• Show the children where to place their offerings on the worship table.

SAY: Our Bible story today is about a special day called Pentecost.

• Point out the Bible Verse Picture, and say the Bible verse for the child.

Picture the Bible Story

Supplies: Leader Guide—p. 90, crayons or markers

• Photocopy "Pentecost" for each child.

• Give each child a copy of the picture.

SAY: Our Bible story is about a special day called Pentecost. The followers of Jesus were all together inside one house. Suddenly, they heard a loud noise and felt a rushing wind. When the followers heard the noise and felt the wind, they knew God was with them.

• Let the children decorate their pictures with crayons or markers. Encourage the children to draw flames over the people in the picture.

Bible Puzzle

Supplies: Bible Story Leaflet—Session 14, p. 4; red crayons or markers

• Give each child a copy of "It's Pentecost."

• Encourage the children to follow the directions to color the Pentecost picture.

SAY: Our Bible story is about a special day called Pentecost. The followers of Jesus were all together inside one house. Suddenly, they heard a loud noise and felt a rushing wind. When the followers heard the noise and felt the wind, they knew God was with them.

Bible Play

Supplies: sand table or sand, shallow tray, plastic tub, or box lid; paper or plastic table covering

• If you do not have a sand table, pour clean sand into a shallow tray, plastic tub, or box lid. Place the sand on a paper or plastic table covering.

• Show the children how to draw a simple fish outline in the sand.

SAY: It was dangerous to be a Christian, and sometimes they had to hide to stay safe. The Christians used a secret picture to tell other Christians who they were. They would draw a simple fish in the dirt or sand.

Into the Bible

Time for the Bible Story

- Have the children follow you to your story area. Sing the following song as you lead the children. The song is sung to the tune of "God Is So Good."

SING: They were all filled,
they were all filled,
they were all filled
with the Holy Spirit.

- Have the children sit down.

SAY: We just sang our Bible verse. Let's say it together: "They were all filled with the Holy Spirit" (Acts 2:4).

Open the Bible

Supplies: Bible Basics Storybook—pp. 262–263

- Tell the children the story, "Pentecost."

Experience the Bible Story

Supplies: CEB Bible; Bible Story Leaflet—Session 14, pp. 2–3; scissors; red, orange, and yellow crepe paper streamers or ribbons

- Cut twelve-inch streamers from red, orange, and yellow crepe paper streamers or ribbon. Group one red, one orange, and one yellow streamer together for each child. Twist one end of the streamers together and wrap the twisted end with tape.

TODAY'S BIBLE TOOL: Stories about people who followed Jesus are in the New Testament.

SAY: Our Bible is divided into two parts, the Old Testament and the New Testament. Stories about Jesus and people who followed Jesus are in the New Testament.

- Show the children the beginning of the New Testament. Then show the children the Book of Acts. Turn to the second chapter.

SAY: Our Bible story is about what happened to the followers of Jesus on a special day called Pentecost. The story is chapter two in the Book of Acts. You will use these streamers as I tell you the story.

- Give each child a set of streamers.

- Place the Leaflet in your Bible. Tell the children the story, "Pentecost" from the Bible Story Leaflet. Encourage them to repeat the sounds and wave the streamers.

ASK: How do you think the followers of Jesus felt when they heard the wind and saw the fire? How does it make you feel to know that God is always with you?

Say the Bible Verse

Supplies: Class Pack—p. 9, Leader Guide—p. 95

- Show the children the Bible Verse Picture. Repeat the verse for the children.

- Teach the children signs from American Sign Language (Leader Guide) to go along with the verse. Encourage the children to make the signs as they say the verse again.

Bible Connections

Pentecost Hats

Supplies: red, orange, and yellow construction paper; red, orange, and yellow crayons or markers; scissors; glue or stapler and staples; tape

- Cut red construction paper into 2 1/2-by-11 strips. Each child will need two strips.
- Cut red, orange, and yellow construction paper into 2-by-4 squares. Or cut the paper into small flame shapes.

SAY: Our Bible story is about a special day called Pentecost. The followers of Jesus were all together inside one house. Suddenly, they heard a loud noise and felt a rushing wind. Then they saw lights like flames flickering above each person's head. Let's make Pentecost hats to remind us of the flames the followers of Jesus saw.

- Give each child two red strips. Tape the two strips together end-to-end to make one long strip. Let the child decorate the strip with red, orange, and yellow crayons or markers.
- Give each child the red, orange, and yellow squares or flame shapes to make paper flames.
- Invite the children to glue, tape, or staple the flames onto the longer red strip. Where the children place the flames will become the front of the hats. If you use staples, make sure the prongs face away from the child's forehead.
- Measure the long strip around the child's head and tape the ends together. Encourage the children to wear their Pentecost hats for the rest of the session.

SAY: When the followers heard the noise, felt the wind, and saw the flames, they knew God was with them.

Pentecost Tag

Supplies: none

SAY: Peter spoke to the crowd and told them about Jesus. Over three thousand people became followers of Jesus on Pentecost. Let's play Pentecost Tag. We're going to pretend we are some of the first followers of Jesus. In this game of tag, we're going to keep adding people to our church.

- Choose a child to be "Peter."
- Have the other children move around the room. Have Peter try to tag a child. When a child is tagged, have the child hold hands with Peter. The two children holding hands become the "church." Now "the church" works together to try to tag another child.
- Have "the church" continue tagging children until everyone is part of the church.
- Choose another child to be Peter, and play the game again.

Live the Bible

Pentecost Party

Supplies: birthday cake or cupcakes, paper plates, napkins, hand-washing supplies, plastic forks, knife (adult use only)

- Prepare or purchase a birthday cake or cupcakes. If possible, choose cake with red decorations.
- Have the children wash their hands.

SAY: Today is Pentecost. We call Pentecost the birthday of the church.

- Choose children to hand out plates and napkins. Show the children the birthday cake or cupcakes. Have the children sing, "Happy Birthday," to the church.

PRAY: Thank you, God, for Pentecost. Thank you for our church. Amen.

- Enjoy the Pentecost snack.

Pentecost Praise

Supplies: streamers used during the Bible story

- Give each child a set of streamers.
- Say the poem printed below and encourage the children to wave their streamers.

Pentecost, Pentecost.
It's a special day.

Pentecost, Pentecost.
Let's make the streamers sway.
(Wave your streamers back and forth.)

Pentecost, Pentecost.
Now wave the streamers high.
(Wave your streamers up in the air.)

Pentecost, Pentecost.
Now listen as we cry.
Happy birthday, church!
(Shout, "Happy birthday, church!")

Express Praise

Praise and Pray

Supplies: CD-ROM, CD player

- Sing with the children the song, "Hear Us As We Pray," from the CD-ROM.
- Encourage the children to name any prayer requests.

PRAY: Thank you, God, for Pentecost, the birthday of the church. Amen.

Blessing

Supplies: Leader Guide—p. 95

- Teach the children the American Sign Language sign for *spirit* (p. 95). Go to each child and sign the word *spirit*.

SAY: *(Child's name),* may God's Spirit be with you.

- Continue until you have blessed each child.

Pentecost

They were all filled with the Holy Spirit. (Acts 2:4)

The B-I-B-L-E
Theme Song

The B-I-B-L-E
Yes, that's the book for me.
I stand alone on the Word of God.
The B-I-B-L-E

B-I-B-L-E (4x)

It starts in Genesis with the Creation
And ends when Jesus returns in Revelation.
And in between the greatest story ever told,
Of Jesus' love for you and me that never lets us go.

Open up the Word, and you'll see
God's plan for you and me.

The B-I-B-L-E, B-I-B-L-E
I stand alone on the Word of God.
The B-I-B-L-E
The B-I-B-L-E, B-I-B-L-E
I stand alone on the Word of God.
The B-I-B-L-E

For every tongue and tribe, for every nation,
It's the gospel of the one who brings salvation.
And one day every knee will bow before the throne.
Until then we've been given everything we need to know.

Open up the Word, and you'll see
God's plan for you and me.

The B-I-B-L-E, B-I-B-L-E
I stand alone on the Word of God.
The B-I-B-L-E
The B-I-B-L-E, B-I-B-L-E
I stand alone on the Word of God.
The B-I-B-L-E

Let's get back to the basics, back to the word,
Back to the greatest news the world's ever heard.
Back to the basics, back to the word,
Back to the greatest news the world's ever heard.

B-I-B-I-B-L-E

The B-I-B-L E, B-I-B-L-E
I stand alone on the Word of God.
The B-I-B-L-E
The B-I-B-L-E, B-I-B-L-E
I stand alone on the Word of God.
The B-I-B-L-E

Words: Andrew Wilson
© 2019 Andrew Wilson. Used by permission.
All rights reserved.

Hear Us As We Pray
Prayer Song

Lord, we call to you right now.
Hear us as we pray.

Folded hands and quiet hearts
Hear us as we pray.

Give us heroes' hearts.
Reveal your truth today.
Give us strength to do what's good.
Hear us as we pray.
Hear us as we pray.

Lord, we ask this in your name.
Hear us as we pray.

Boldly share, your truth proclaim.
Hear us as we pray.

Give us heroes' hearts
To live your truth each day.
Give us courage in our faith.
Hear us as we pray.
Hear us as we pray.

Lord, we call to you right now.
Hear us as we pray.

Guide our feet and light our way.
Hear us as we pray.

Give us heroes' hearts
In all we do and say.
Give us hope as we seek peace.
Hear us as we pray.
Hear us as we pray.

Hear us as we pray.

Words: Matt Huesmann
© 2017 Matt Huesmann Music. Used by permission.
All rights reserved.

Psalm 121:8

Unit 1 Bible Verse Signs

The LORD will **protect you** on your **journeys**—whether going or coming.

Lord

Hold your right index finger and right thumb in an *L* shape. Place the *L* on your left shoulder, and then move the *L* across your body to your right waist.

Protect

Hold both hands chest high, with your hands flat. Make an *X* with your flat hands.

You

Point an index finger away from yourself.

Journeys

Partially bend your right index finger and your middle finger, and hold your right hand in front of your body. Move your right hand up in a zigzag line.

Matthew 28:7

Unit 2 Bible Verse Signs

Now **hurry, go** and tell his disciples, "**He's** been **raised** from the **dead**."

Hurry

Make fists with both hands, and stick your index and middle fingers out straight from the fists. Hold your hands in front of your body. Move your hands quickly up and down.

Go

Point both of your index fingers away from yourself in one quick movement.

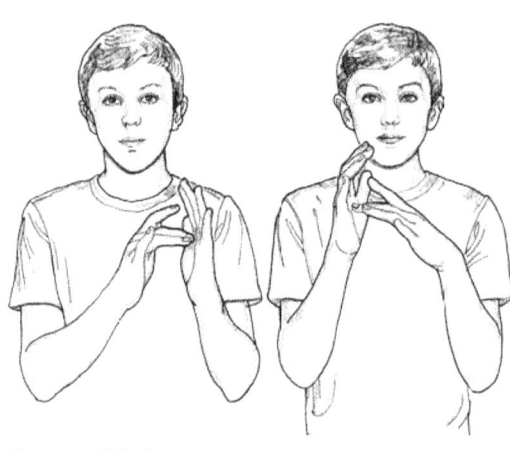

Jesus (He)

Touch the middle finger of your right hand to the palm of your left hand, and then touch the middle finger of your left hand to the palm of your right hand.

Raised

Make fists with both hands, and stick your index and middle fingers out straight from the fists. Hold both hands in front of your body, with your left palm facing up and your right palm facing down. Flip your left hand and place the fingers extended from your left hand on top of the fingers extended from your right hand.

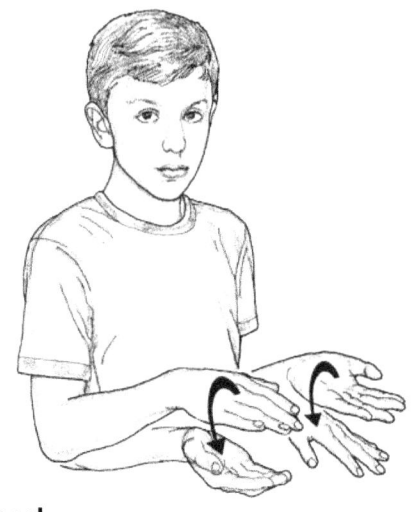

Dead

Hold both of your hands in front of your body. Your left palm should be facing up, and your right palm should be facing down. Flip both hands. Your left palm should now be facing down, and your right palm should now be facing up.

Permission is granted to duplicate this page for local church use only. © 2019 Abingdon Press.

Acts 2:4

Unit 3 Bible Verse Signs

They were all **filled** with the Holy **Spirit**.

They

Point your right index finger. Make a small sweeping motion with your right hand.

Filled

Make a fist with your right hand. Hold your right hand in front of your body. Swip over the top of your right fist with your left palm.

Spirit

Touch your index finger to your thumb on both hands. Hold your left hand palm facing up. Touch the thumb and index finger of your left hand to the thumb and index finger of your right hand and then move your right hand up in a small circular motions.

Comments from Users

Let us know what you think! Your comments will help us write a better curriculum for you and the children you teach. Please send your comments and suggestions to:

Daphna Flegal, Children's Unit
The United Methodist Publishing House
2222 Rosa L. Parks Blvd.
Nashville, TN 37228-1306

Please check the components that you use:

_____ Leader Guide
_____ Bible Story Leaflets
_____ Class Pack
_____ Student Take-Home CD
_____ Bible Basics Storybook

Use the following scale to rate each of the resources:
N/A = Not Applicable
1 = Never
2 = Sometimes
3 = Most of the Time
4 = All of the Time

Leader Guide

_____ The Leader Guide was easy to use.
_____ Children grew to understand the Bible stories from the suggested activities.

Comments about Leader Guide:
_____
_____
_____

Bible Story Leaflets

_____ The children enjoyed moving to the Bible stories as they were read to them.

Comments about Bible Story Leaflets:
_____
_____
_____

Class Pack

_____ The Bible verse pictures were colorful and engaging for the children.
_____ We used the Attendance Chart.

Student Take-Home CD

_____ The children enjoyed learning and singing the songs on the CD.

Bible Basics Storybook

_____ The children enjoyed hearing the retellings of the Bible stories.

My favorite activity this quarter was _____
_____
_____

My least favorite activity this quarter was _____
_____
_____

Overall, I would rate this **Spring 2020** quarter:
_____

3 = The best that it could possibly be.
2 = Provided some good moments for the children's faith development.
1 = Ineffective with the faith development of the children in my church.

Leader's Name: _____
Church: _____
Address: _____
_____
Phone No.: _____

Permission is granted to duplicate this page for local church use only. © 2019 Abingdon Press.

Building a better world through God's story

Bible Basics Storybook invites your children into God's story with 149 core stories from both the Old and New Testaments. Also includes colorful illustrations and prayers to start the day, to say at bedtime, and to share before meals, which will help you provide a solid faith foundation for the dear children in your life.

Not only is *Bible Basics Storybook* a great addition to your classroom, it's perfect for families with young children to use at home as they explore God's story together. *Abingdon Press.*

9781501881497. **Hardcover.** $19.99; **$15.99**

Prices subject to change. For most current pricing, call or visit Cokesbury.com.

800-672-1789 | Cokesbury.com
Call a Resource Consultant

 | Spring Year 1
Vol. 1 • No. 3

EDITORIAL / DESIGN TEAM

Daphna Flegal . . . . Writer/Editor
Julie P. Glass . . . . Production Editor
Jim Carlton . . . . Designer

ADMINISTRATIVE TEAM

Rev. Brian K. Milford . . . . President and Publisher
Marjorie M. Pon . . . . Associate Publisher and Editor of Church School Publications (CSP)
Mary M. Mitchell . . . . Design Manager
Brittany Sky . . . . Senior Editor, Children's Resources

BIBLE STORY BASICS: PRE-READER, LEADER GUIDE: An official resource for The United Methodist Church approved by Discipleship Ministries and published quarterly by Abingdon Press, a division of The United Methodist Publishing House, 2222 Rosa L. Parks Blvd., Nashville, TN 37228-1306. Price: $14.99. Copyright © 2019 Abingdon Press. All rights reserved. Send address changes to BIBLE STORY BASICS: PRE-READER, LEADER GUIDE, Subscription Services, 2222 Rosa L. Parks Blvd., Nashville, TN 37228-1306 or call 800-672-1789. Printed in the United States of America.

To order copies of this publication, call toll free: **800-672-1789**. You may fax your order to 800-445-8189. Telecommunication Device for the Deaf/Telex Telephone: 800-227-4091. Or order online at *cokesbury.com*. Use your Cokesbury account, American Express, Visa, Discover, or Mastercard.

For information concerning permission to reproduce any material in this publication, write to Rights and Permissions, The United Methodist Publishing House, 2222 Rosa L. Parks Blvd., Nashville, TN 37228-1306. You may fax your request to 615-749-6128. Or email *permissions@umpublishing.org*.

Scripture quotations are taken from the Common English Bible, copyright 2011. Used by permission. All rights reserved.

PACP10557325-01

www.ingramcontent.com/pod-product-compliance
Lightning Source LLC
LaVergne TN
LVHW061314060426
835507LV00019B/2157